BLOOMERS AND BALLOTS

*Elizabeth Cady Stanton
and Women's Rights*

"My life has been one long struggle to do and say what I know to be right and true. I would not take back one brave word or deed. My only regret is that I have not been braver and bolder and truer in uttering the honest conviction of my soul."

ELIZABETH CADY STANTON
June 1, 1860

MARY STETSON CLARKE

Bloomers and Ballots

ELIZABETH CADY STANTON
AND WOMEN'S RIGHTS

The Viking Press   New York

For my nieces
Barbara
and
Sarah
Stetson

First Edition

Copyright © 1972 by Mary Stetson Clarke. All rights reserved. First
published in 1972 by The Viking Press, Inc., 625 Madison Avenue,
New York, N.Y. 10022. Published simultaneously in Canada by The
Macmillan Company of Canada Limited.
SBN 670-17437-8
Library of Congress catalog card number: 72–80523
Printed in U.S.A.
920 S   1. Stanton, Elizabeth Cady
         2. Women's Rights

1   2   3   4   5   76   75   74   73   72

CONTENTS

Elizabeth Cady Stanton at the age of twenty

1

WHAT IS TRULY RIGHT ?

With a pitiless disregard for snarls, Nurse drew the stiff brush firmly through Elizabeth's brown curls. Although she felt like crying out in pain, Elizabeth stood quiet and tense, a sturdy little figure in a red calico dress and starched white pinafore. The less she complained the sooner Nurse would finish, and she might then go out to play.

An August breeze fanned the curtains at the nursery's open windows. From the yard below came the voices of her sisters, Madge and Kate, aged six and four. They were younger than Elizabeth, who had reached the age of eight, and she sometimes felt too old to enter into their games. Perhaps Dr. Hosack, their next-door neighbor, would be in his garden this afternoon. Then she could have one of her long talks with the elderly clergyman about things that puzzled her.

Was that the sound of his spade striking against a stone? She turned her head to look out the window, and felt a tug on her hair, so sharp that it brought tears to her eyes.

"Can't you stand still for even one minute?" Nurse demanded.

Elizabeth did not need to look up to see the stern Scottish face with its thin mouth and frowning brows.

"I only wanted to see if Dr. Hosack was in his garden," Elizabeth explained.

"Whether he is or not won't matter to you today," Nurse

said tartly. "You must stay in this afternoon to work on your sampler."

Work on her sampler? If there was anything Elizabeth hated doing, it was poking her needle into the piece of linen marked with the alphabet; her name, Elizabeth Smith Cady; and the year, 1824. She had to strain her eyes trying to make each little cross match the others. She pricked her fingers and broke her thread. And all she ever had for her pains was a headache.

"Why must I stay in?" she demanded. "Madge and Kate are playing outdoors."

"Because you have been a naughty girl three times this week."

Elizabeth's blue eyes flashed. Her pink cheeks flushed rosier than ever. "I didn't mean to be," she said.

"But you were," Nurse stated. "Yesterday you took a cake to the jail and gave it to the prisoners. A fine thing that was for a young lady like you!"

I was only trying to be kind, Elizabeth thought. Didn't the Bible say that one should feed the hungry?

Yesterday morning she had played with the daughter of the county sheriff, whose residence and the jail adjoined the County Courthouse, one block away from the Cady house on Main Street in Johnstown, New York. With her friend, Elizabeth had gone into the jail, talked with the prisoners in their cells, and carried food to them at noon. Back home at the dinner table, Elizabeth could not help contrasting her own delicious meal with the prisoners' rough fare. From the well-stocked pantry she had taken a cake, which she and her playmate distributed to the jail's inmates.

"The prisoners needed something good to eat. Just think, they will have to stay in jail until court is held in October!"

"What happens to the prisoners is no concern of yours," Nurse snapped.

Elizabeth sighed. She could never make Nurse understand how sorry she felt for other people. When she looked at the men behind bars, she thought how terrible it would be if Father were so confined. Of course, Father would never be in jail. He was the most respected person in Johnstown. But if he should ever come to such a pass, she would take cakes to him every day. For a moment she felt again the glow of happiness she had experienced when the men thanked her for their treat.

"Then on Wednesday you talked with that boy who has no arms," Nurse continued relentlessly.

"It isn't Billy's fault that he was born so. It's because his father was a terrible drunkard. I heard Cook say so," Elizabeth declared.

"Tut tut. What kind of talk is that?" Nurse shook her head in reproof. "You shouldn't pay attention to such a cripple."

Elizabeth turned her head away. Every time she thought of poor Billy she nearly wept. But he, surprisingly, was always cheerful. How could he be so? That was one of the things she wanted to ask Dr. Hosack about. He was wise and kind and took great pains to answer her questions seriously. When he was in his garden, digging or hoeing, dressed in old, stained clothing, it was hard to realize he was the same man who preached about Hell's fires and everlasting damnation from the pulpit of the Presbyterian Church.

Perhaps he could tell her why a boy so handicapped as Billy could have a disposition so happy.

"And Sunday morning," Nurse went on accusingly, "you went with Peter to the early service at the Episcopal Church." Her tone was icy with disapproval.

"Mother said I could go," Elizabeth said hastily.

"But what did you do when you were there? I heard it all from a friend. You turned your back on the usher and sat with Peter—a servant!"

"I had to," Elizabeth explained. "Mr. Meade wouldn't let Peter go up front with me. So I had to take the back pew with him. You wouldn't expect me to sit with anyone else, would you?"

Even now she could feel the surprise and anger that had gripped her when the stout, bald man with pink cheeks and white side whiskers had waved her to a pew and then blocked Peter's passage. She had slipped under Mr. Meade's outstretched arm and followed Peter back down the aisle so closely that his swinging coattails had almost brushed her flaming cheeks. She would never forget the expression of amazement and pleasure that had flooded over his face when he reached the hindmost pew, turned to go in, and saw her. He had stopped stock-still, smiled at her, and stepped aside to let her precede him. She had known then that what she had done was right. How could Nurse turn it into something wrong?

"You should have sat anywhere but in the Negro pew," Nurse stormed.

"Why?" Elizabeth asked.

"Because you are the daughter of Mr. Daniel Cady, the most important lawyer and gentleman in Johnstown and all this part of New York State. You must learn that you have a position in life."

"But Peter is my friend. Next to Father and Dr. Hosack I love him best of all the men I know."

The nurse glared at Elizabeth. "Peter is your father's servant, and has been for over twenty years. Besides, he is *black!*" Her tone was laden with contempt.

Of course Peter was black. He was also very handsome, dignified, and capable. No one could welcome guests to the Cady home more graciously than Peter, standing tall and straight in his blue coat with brass buttons. There was nothing Peter could not do, from driving a team of horses to coaxing the kitchen fire back to life, or playing a tune on his fiddle that made Elizabeth want to dance forever.

Nurse marched to the tall chest between the windows, yanked open a drawer, and drew forth Elizabeth's sampler. "Here," she said, putting the rumpled square into Elizabeth's hands. "See that you put your stitches in evenly." Taking up a basket of mending, she seated herself on the opposite side of the room and began to darn stockings.

Elizabeth threaded her needle and commenced the letter G. Would she ever get through the entire alphabet? The thread knotted. She tried to untangle it, and broke the silk. Suddenly the needle jabbed into her finger. Ouch! She wiped the blood on her pinafore.

At last the G was finished. Springing to her feet, Elizabeth flung the limp square in Nurse's lap and cried, "Now may I go out?"

Squinting, Nurse held the work at arm's length. Then she pressed her lips together. "No, you must do another letter."

At the words, Elizabeth's pent-up rebellion burst forth.

"All you ever say to me is *no*," she stormed in anguish. "It's all I ever hear. And in church it's the same. Even the Commandments begin 'Thou shalt not!' "

For a moment Nurse stared in open-mouthed astonishment. Then she stood up so abruptly that her lapful of stockings fell to the floor. "I've had more than I can stand. It's bad enough when you are disobedient. But when you talk against the Holy Scriptures—that's something else. Come along. I shall take you to your mother."

Fearfully Elizabeth followed Nurse, watching her starched white apron strings dance over her long black skirt. Being taken to Mother was the thing she dreaded most when she had been naughty. Mother was so beautiful and dignified that Elizabeth could not bear to disappoint her.

Outside the open windows of the long upper hallway the elm trees threw cool shade. Down in the garden Madge and Kate were serving fairy tea in hollyhock cups. Dr. Hosack was smiling at them over the low hedge between the gardens. If only she might be out there, too!

But here she was, going down the staircase to the entrance hall, past the parlor's dim shadows to the sunlit sitting room. Mother was standing at the round center table, turning over samples of fabric. On either side were Elizabeth's older sisters, Tryphena, nineteen, and Harriet, thirteen. Tryphena was tall, like Mother, with the same dark, curly hair and even features. Hattie was short, like Elizabeth, with blue eyes and light brown hair.

"Which material would you like for your new ball gown, the blue satin or the rose brocade?" Mother asked Tryphena.

Lucky Tryphena! She could choose what she would wear, while Elizabeth must always be dressed in red like her younger sisters, as if they were three crimson elves. It was unfair to be treated so.

Tryphena was looking at Elizabeth critically. "I suppose Lizzie has been getting into mischief again," she said coldly. "Oh, look, she's got blood on her pinafore. How messy!"

Elizabeth looked down guiltily. Tryphena was right, as usual. If only she wouldn't act so superior.

"Did you hurt yourself?" Harriet asked sympathetically.

Elizabeth held out her finger, squeezing it until the blood ran.

"Ooh, those needle pricks can hurt," Harriet said.

Mother put aside the cloth and looked at Nurse. "Did you wish to speak to me?" she inquired.

While Elizabeth stood mute and miserable, Nurse launched into a recital of the week's misdemeanors. When she had finished, Mother said, "I am sorry that Elizabeth has caused you difficulty. You may leave her with me. I am sure you have other matters to attend to now."

As soon as the Scotswoman had left, Elizabeth burst out passionately, "I hate Nurse! I wish she would go away and never come back."

"She is here to teach you to behave properly," Mrs. Cady said equably.

"I don't want to be proper. I want to be me!" Elizabeth declared.

Just then Nelly, the housemaid, appeared. "The ladies from the church are here for the meeting, ma'am," she announced.

Mrs. Cady looked at the clock on the wall. "Oh, dear, four o'clock already. Show them into the parlor, Nelly, and tell them I'll be there directly." She gestured toward the samples. "Try to make up your minds about materials, girls." Then she put a hand on Elizabeth's shoulder. "And you, my tempestuous little daughter, come with me."

Trembling, Elizabeth obeyed. What was going to happen to her now? Suddenly she was overwhelmed by the magnitude of her sins. Not only had she committed all the evils Nurse had outlined, but she had said she hated Nurse.

Mother's long fingers felt cool to Elizabeth's small, perspiring hand. As they walked along the hall toward the front of the house, her spirits began to lift. Mother must be going to take her to Father's office, as she had many times before. Elizabeth's anxiety began to ebb. Of course it was hard to be kept indoors on a sunny day, but to have all Father's attention, even in reprimand, was a privilege worth suffering any scolding to achieve.

As they passed the vestibule, the front door burst open and in stepped Elizabeth's only brother, Eleazer. He wore riding clothes and carried a crop in one hand. His cheeks were flushed and his hair was blown in wavy locks on either side of his thin, sensitive face. Elizabeth looked up at him adoringly. No one in her world seemed so exalted as Eleazer, eighteen years old and a student at Union College, now home for a brief vacation. After graduation he would enter into the practice of law with Father.

Leaning forward, Eleazer kissed his mother on the cheek and swept the top of his crop across Elizabeth's curls. "Hello, moppet," he said fondly.

"Did you have a good ride?" Margaret Cady asked.

"Capital. Out in the woods behind Johnson Hall to see the new property Father just bought."

"You must tell us about it at dinner. Right now I have a meeting with some church women in the parlor."

Eleazer ran up the stairs, two at a time. Elizabeth and Mother went down the corridor that led to Father's office adjoining the house. Mother gave her special knock—three short raps, a pause, then one more.

Stepping past the heavy oak door into the office was like entering another world, Elizabeth thought. At the far end of the room was a long table strewn with piles of papers where one of Father's law students was working. Beside it was a tall writing desk at which another young man was scratching away with one of the popular new steel pens on a sheet of foolscap. Still another lawyer in training was consulting a thick, leather-bound volume from the shelves that covered the walls.

Father sat at his desk, taking notes from an open book. He sprang to his feet, tall and spare, and walked toward them with a quick step. "To what do I owe the honor of this visitation?" he inquired with a smile.

"Nurse has brought Elizabeth to me for discipline. I cannot take the time to talk with her now. I wonder if an hour here in your office might not have a salutary effect?"

"What was her offense?" Daniel Cady asked.

"Nurse says she was disobedient," Mother replied. She hurried away.

Daniel Cady bent his gaze upon Elizabeth. One eye had a gray film over it from an injury in early manhood. The

other was so keen it seemed to pierce through Elizabeth's
skull deep into her mind. "Were you disobedient?" His tone
was gentle.

"Ye-es, I suppose so. But I didn't *know* I was doing
wrong."

Father nodded sympathetically. "Unfortunately, ignorance of the law is no excuse," he said slowly. "You will
have to learn what is right and what is wrong, and behave
accordingly."

Elizabeth listened intently. Father often talked to her as if
she were a woman grown. He was sometimes hard to understand, but he was always fair.

"Some of the things that Nurse says are wrong seem to
me to be *right*," she said.

Father nodded his head in agreement. "Just so. There are
people older than you who believe that some of our nation's
laws are wrong. But that does not give them the right to
break those laws."

"What should they do?" Elizabeth asked.

"They should take steps to see that new and better laws
are enacted," Daniel Cady said.

A knock sounded on the outside door. Elizabeth's spirits
sank. It must be a client to see Father. Now he would turn
his attention from her to the newcomer. A shiver of dread
ran through her. What if the caller was a woman? Would
she, like other women Elizabeth had seen on previous occasions, lay her problem before Father only to be told that
there was no legal way in which he could help her? All too
clearly Elizabeth could recall the scenes, each played by different female characters, each with the same sad ending. Father, like a figure of doom, would take down from the shelf

a large volume, turn to a passage, and say regretfully, "I am sorry, but there is nothing I can do to assist you. The law clearly states that a married woman has no legal position in such a case."

Then he would read from the volume a statute that caused the woman to blanch in dismay. Elizabeth was so troubled over the sorrow of these women that she had made a secret plan to come to the office some day when Father was away. She would take the scissors and cut out every one of the laws that so distressed the women. She would know which laws to remove because she had quietly marked them after Father read them aloud.

To Elizabeth's relief, the newcomer was a man asking for Mr. Cady's opinion on a boundary dispute.

Father led Elizabeth to a low chair in a corner a short distance from his desk. "Sit down here, Elizabeth, and think over what we have been discussing."

Soon Father and the client were deep in conversation over property titles. Elizabeth paid no attention to their low voices. She leaned back in her chair and let her gaze wander around the room, to the young men busy about their duties, and the shrubs' green branches waving outside the windows. The office was cool and peaceful. This is the nicest part of the house, she decided.

Father's words came back to her. He had said that some people thought that laws should be changed. If laws needed changing, how could anyone tell what was truly right and what was wrong? It was all very puzzling.

The neighbor left, a pleased expression on his face. Father must have been of help to him.

For a few minutes the office was silent except for the

turning of pages and the scratching of pens. Then another knock sounded.

When the visitor stepped over the threshold, Elizabeth's heart sank, although she knew and liked the newcomer. It was Mrs. Flora Campbell, who came to the back door every Saturday with a basket of farm produce. Just last week she had brought fresh lettuce, eggs, and plump chickens, neatly plucked, resting on a bed of grape leaves. In one corner of her basket had been tucked a little squash shaped like a tiny snowman. She had given it to Elizabeth for a toy.

Today Flora's eyes were red, her cheek bore a purple bruise, and the corners of her mouth were drawn down with sorrow. She stood diffidently in the doorway until Mr. Cady ushered her to the chair beside his desk.

"I was sorry to hear of the death of your husband. He was a fine man," Mr. Cady said.

Flora put her handkerchief to her eyes. "There never was a better. Ah, but he'd turn over in his grave if he could know what's happened now that he's gone."

"What is the trouble?" Mr. Cady asked.

"It's that stepson of mine, a lazy good-for-nothing who can't leave liquor alone."

Elizabeth knew and feared Jock Campbell. He was a heavy-set, beefy-faced fellow, usually idling about town. When he staggered out the tavern door, even the big boys got out of his way. Elizabeth was sure he was responsible for the bruise on Flora's cheek.

"In all his life he's done naught to keep the farm going and has drunk up every penny he could get his paws on," Flora said. "Now he has the gall to say all my property belongs to him, every stick and stone of it. What's more, he says that he owns the house now, and that I'm to move out of it. I want you to set him right, Mr. Cady."

Father's voice was very low. "In what way, Mrs. Campbell?"

"I want you to tell him that the farm is mine, that it came to me when my father died, before ever I was married." Flora bent her troubled gaze on the lawyer.

"Yes, I remember. I handled the details."

"Then you can tell him that it's mine!" Flora leaned back in relief.

Mr. Cady cleared his throat. "You know that when you married, the farm became the property of your husband?"

"Yes. But now he's dead, so it's mine again."

Mr. Cady put the tips of his fingers together and looked at them fixedly. "I'm afraid that's not correct," he said slowly. "The law says that when a man dies, his property goes to his legal heir. In this case his heir is Jock, his son by his first marriage."

Flora Campbell stared in astonishment. "Do you mean to say that Jock is right—that the farm is legally his?"

"I'm afraid so," Mr. Cady said.

"And the house? The only home I've ever known?"

"Yes, the house, too." Mr. Cady rose, went to the bookshelves, and reached down a thick volume. "Here is the law. You may read it for yourself."

Slowly Flora studied the words, then blurted, "That may be the law, but it's not right!" She hid her face in her workworn hands for a few minutes. Then she lifted her tearstained countenance and exclaimed, "Oh, Mr. Cady, I never thought I'd see the day when I'd be fallen so low." Her lined face contorted, she departed abruptly.

Poor Flora Campbell! Elizabeth ran from the office and caught up with the woman at the gate. "Don't worry," she said, coming to a sudden decision. "Everything is going to be all right. On Sunday when Father is in church, I'm going to cut that wicked law out of the book. Then it can't hurt you any more."

That evening after dessert, as Father neatly rolled his linen napkin and inserted it in its silver ring, he said, "Elizabeth, I want you to come into my office."

To be singled out thus was very unusual. Elizabeth looked first at Mother, then at Nurse, for some clue. She could discover none. Her mind raced back over the day. Was Father going to reprimand her for leaving his office without permission? Trembling, she followed him to the book-lined room, shadowy in the twilight. He shut the door and motioned her to the visitor's chair beside his desk. Breathlessly she waited.

"We started to talk about laws this afternoon," he said. "Now I think it is time that you learned how laws are made."

Elizabeth listened carefully as he told how a bill was proposed, voted upon, and signed. He went on to explain how the law was then printed, included in lawbooks, and distributed to lawyers and libraries all over the country.

A spark of alarm flickered in Elizabeth's mind. Had Father guessed her plan? His quiet voice went on.

"No matter what might happen to the books in my office, if they were burned in a fire or blown apart in an explosion, the laws would remain the same. My books are only a few of many thousands which record the laws. And even if every volume should be destroyed, the laws would still be laws.

Do you understand, my dear?" His smile was very gentle.

Elizabeth could feel the blood rushing to her cheeks. Father had guessed her secret. More likely, Flora Campbell had told him of her intent. Chagrin, and then relief flooded over her. Thank goodness she had not cut out the pages. She would not have accomplished her purpose and would surely have displeased Father. Deeply troubled, she asked, "Is there anything I can do to change laws that hurt women like Flora Campbell?"

For a few moments Daniel Cady was silent. Then he said, "If you were a boy with the prospect of voting at the age of twenty-one, I would advise you to run for the legislature and introduce bills to give married women the right to own property. But as a woman you will not have a part in lawmaking."

Why should women not have a right to make or change laws that vitally affected them? It was not fair! Elizabeth was about to protest, but Father was still speaking, and he must never be interrupted.

"However, you could try to persuade the men in office to change the laws. When you are grown up and able to prepare a speech, you could go to Albany and talk to the members of the legislature. You could tell them about the women who come into this office and the laws that are unfair to them. If you should covince the legislators to pass new laws, the old ones would no longer be in force."

So there was a way for her to help Flora Campbell and the other poor women who had come to Father! A way that was right and proper. Elizabeth momentarily forgot her indignation that women could take no part in lawmaking.

Then another thought flashed into her mind. What about

the rules that Nurse had punished her for breaking? Could
Father tell her how to change them? Breathlessly she recited
her misdemeanors, then asked, "Will it ever be right for me
to visit prisoners in jail? Or talk to cripples? Or sit beside
black people?"

Father gave her a puzzled glance. "Why do you trouble
yourself about such matters, Elizabeth? Let older heads than
yours decide what is right. All you must do is be obedient,
learn your lessons, and grow up into a fine woman like your
mother so that someday you may have a home and children
of your own."

A few moments later Elizabeth closed the heavy office
door behind her, and stood motionless in the corridor. Father's good-night kiss was cool upon her forehead, and his
words still echoed in her ears. She should be pleased to have
had so much of Father's time and attention. Instead she felt
bewildered and disappointed.

When she had questioned Father about a way to correct
laws that were unfair to women, he had given her a straight-
forward answer. But when she had asked him about the
treatment of prisoners, cripples, and Negroes, he had not answered her at all. He had merely repeated what she had
heard a hundred times from other grownups about being
good and learning her lessons. As for growing up to have a
home and children of her own, Elizabeth was not sure that
she looked forward to the prospect. Mother's life seemed
dull and unexciting compared with Father's.

Slowly Elizabeth made her way along the passage. At
least she was certain of one thing. Someday, as Father had
suggested, she would make a speech to aid women like Flora
Campbell. And someday, too, she would make it right and

proper to show kindness to people in jails or with crippled bodies or black skins. If Father could not tell her how, she would find a way herself.

2

"IF ONLY YOU WERE
A BOY!"

*T*wo years later, on another August afternoon, Elizabeth sat on a straight-backed chair in the front hallway just outside the closed parlor door. Stiff with misery, she fought back the tears that kept welling into her eyes. She was ten years old now, old enough not to cry, although she had never before felt so overwhelmed by sorrow.

Rain streamed against the panes of the vestibule's double doors. A flash of lightning lit with garish intensity a steel engraving of the Roman Forum, hung with white crepe, and a wreath of flowers standing on the hall table. In the glare Elizabeth could read Eleazer's name inscribed on the broad ribbon that stretched diagonally across the wreath.

Why had Eleazer had to die? He had been well and strong on his last vacation from Union College. But when he came home after graduation he had been gravely ill. With fearful rapidity he had grown weaker and weaker until he could no longer leave his bed. The doctor had come and gone; he had prescribed bleedings and medicines. But despite all his treatment Eleazer had worsened steadily.

Day by day the family had watched and waited. Father, after his visits to the sickroom, had paced up and down the upper hall, his usually composed countenance contorted with grief. Mother had remained calm, but she grew pale and drawn.

Very early this morning, when it was scarcely light, Nurse had led Elizabeth, Madge, and Kate to Eleazer's room, where Mother and Father and the two older girls sat around the bed. Eleazer's body was so shrunken that it hardly made a ridge under the bedclothes. Every bone stood out in his emaciated face. His eyes were closed, and he might have been asleep. But the sound of his breathing was like the cry of a wounded bird. Would it echo in her ears forever? Elizabeth wondered.

While the family sat in wordless vigil, the tortured breaths suddenly ceased. Elizabeth listened, waiting for them to begin again, breathless herself in her anxiety. But there was only the silence, and then a sob from Mother as she buried her face in her hands.

Father's face was like a mask. Elizabeth watched him kneel by the bed, and knew that she must do likewise. In a moment they were all on their knees while Father began a prayer for Eleazer's soul, and for the comfort and support of his bereaved family. Father's voice, ordinarily firm and decisive, now faltered and broke.

Poor Father! For twenty years he had looked forward to the day when Eleazer would join him in the practice of law. Now death had ended his dream.

A clap of thunder followed the lightning. Elizabeth put her hands to her ears until the rumbling subsided.

The house seemed very quiet afterward. Upstairs in her bedroom Mother was resting. Tryphena and Harriet were in their rooms, and the younger girls in the nursery. Elizabeth had been there, too, until Nurse had sent her downstairs, saying it was time for her to go and look at her brother in his coffin.

Elizabeth shivered. It had wrenched her heart to look at Eleazer as he lay dying. What possible good could it do for her to look at him now that he was dead? She twisted her hands together. Perhaps if she went back upstairs now Nurse would not ask whether she had obeyed or not.

She was slipping off the chair when from behind the closed door of the parlor there issued a deep groan. For a moment Elizabeth froze in fright. Was that Eleazer's ghost? The servants were forever telling stories of spirits that returned to earth. Would Eleazer be one of those?

The groan came again, and she recognized Father's voice. Dear Father! She must comfort him. Softly she turned the knob, opened the door, and entered.

Inside the room, she blinked in disbelief. The parlor was deep in shadow, its blinds all drawn. White crepe was draped over every picture and mirror. In the center of the room stood the casket, also draped in white. Beside it sat Father, pale and immovable, staring with unseeing eyes.

Elizabeth walked slowly toward him, trying not to think of Eleazer's body lying waxlike in the open coffin. She would think only of Father. He had loved Eleazer more than any of his other children. No wonder he was suffering so deeply.

For a long time she stood in wordless sympathy by his side. At last, overcome by his desolation, she climbed up into his lap and rested her head against his chest. How steady was the beat of his heart. Poor Eleazer's heart was stilled forever. What could she say that would give Father comfort?

As she sat there, leaning against him, she felt his arms go

around her. He gave a sigh that seemed to come from the very depths of his being.

"Oh, my daughter," he cried in anguish, "if only you were a boy!"

Elizabeth blinked back her tears. What did it matter that she was not a boy? She was alive—alive and filled with eagerness to help her grieving parent.

"Don't be sad, Father," she said. "You still have me. I promise to be like a son to you." Tenderly she pressed her cheek to his, expecting some sign of response. There was none, only another groan. Poor Father! He was so sad he may not have understood her, but she would prove to him that she meant what she had promised.

For a few minutes longer she remained in his arms. When his hold relaxed, she slipped down and left the parlor.

All the rest of the day Elizabeth moved about as in a trance. It was not enough that she had promised Father to be like a son. She must prove her intention immediately. What could she do to show him that she would be everything her brother was?

Her mind moved back to the long-ago day when Kate was born. People had said what a pity it was that she was not a boy. Probably they had said the same thing about herself and her other sisters. Why should boys be considered so much better than girls?

Boys could certainly do more things. That was partly because of their superior strength and partly because of their freedom to use their bodies. If girls were allowed to run and climb trees and swim like boys, would they not be as strong?

But she must not let her thoughts wander. She must think

which of the many things Eleazer had done that she might
also do. In memory she pictured Eleazer when he had been
at home. How he and his friends had loved to rise at dawn
and go off on early morning rides over the hills. How handsome they had looked, almost like knights of old. It must be
very exciting to gallop over the countryside.

Suddenly Elizabeth made up her mind. She, too, would
ride horseback. Of course she would have to ride on a sidesaddle, with one knee hooked over the support, a pose that
looked terribly uncomfortable and dangerous. And she
would have to wear a voluminous riding skirt, so long that it
must be held up when she walked. But if she could overcome those obstacles and learn to ride as well as Eleazer, she
might convince Father that girls could be as capable as boys.

In what other way could she be like her brother?

She recalled Eleazer as a student at Johnstown Academy,
where she and her sisters were also enrolled. On warm days
when the windows were open she had heard his class chant-
ing its Greek lesson.

Ah—Greek! For some unfathomable reason only boys
studied the classics. Greek required no physical skill, only
one's brain. Surely her mind was as keen as a boy's, and better than some. She would learn Greek.

But how to learn it? The Academy was closed for the
summer. Even if it were open, there was little chance of her
being allowed to join the boys' class.

All at once she thought of Dr. Hosack's study. She was
certain that she had seen some Greek books on his shelves.
Perhaps he would help her.

Early the next morning, while the rest of the family slept,
Elizabeth crept into the garden and squeezed through the

hedge. Dr. Hosack was cultivating his rosebushes. He looked up at her approach, a sad smile lighting his face. She hoped he would not say any more about Eleazer. Yesterday he had paid a formal call to express his sympathy to the family.

Before he could speak, she asked quickly, "Will you give me Greek lessons, Dr. Hosack? I have promised my father to be like a son to him, and so I must study Greek."

If the clergyman felt any surprise, he did not show it. "I would consider it a privilege," he said in his dignified way.

"May we begin now?" Elizabeth asked eagerly.

Dr. Hosack threw down his hoe. "Indeed we may. Come along."

Elizabeth forgot her dislike of the gloomy parsonage as she tiptoed after Dr. Hosack into his study. He opened a window, letting a wave of fragrant morning air into the musty room, then reached down a worn leather volume from a shelf.

"This is the Greek grammar that I used at the University of Glasgow when I was a student there," he said. "Sit here beside me at my desk, and we shall begin with the Greek alphabet."

"But I know that already," Elizabeth said.

"Upon my soul! And how did you learn it?"

"By hearing the boys recite."

"Let me hear you say it," said the minister.

"Alpha, beta, gamma, delta," Elizabeth began, and continued on, ending with, "chi, psi, and omega."

"Do you know the characters as well?" Dr. Hosack asked.

"No."

"Here they are. Look at them closely, and recite them as I point to each one."

As she scrutinized the Greek characters, Elizabeth could see in some their likeness to the English alphabet she knew so well. In a short time her quick mind had recorded each unfamiliar symbol.

"Now this is the way they sound," Dr. Hosack said. "Gamma is like the g in *good*, epsilon like the *e* in *bet*, and theta like the *th* in *thistle*."

Carefully Elizabeth formed the sounds of each letter, imitating the minister's pronunciation.

"Very good," he said. "Now, the next thing to learn is the Greek article, the Greek for *the*. You are doing so well that I believe we'll have time for it this morning."

Elizabeth sat up very straight, focusing her thoughts on the symbols.

"We have three genders in Greek: the masculine, feminine, and neuter," Dr. Hosack said, "and a singular and a plural. We also have four cases: the nominative, the accusative, the genitive, and the dative."

He pointed to a list of words on the dog-eared page. "This is the singular. Repeat after me, if you please: *Hoe, hee, toe; ton* (as in *on*), *teen, toe; tow* (as in *how*), *teece, tow; toe, tee, toe*. And here is the plural: *Hoy, high, ta; tow, tahs, ta; tone, tone, tone; toice, tice, toice*."

From the back of Elizabeth's memory came a recollection of the same sounds issuing from the boys' classroom at the Johnstown Academy.

"The Greek language is very precise," Dr. Hosack continued. "That is why it requires twenty-four ways of saying *the*. Let's go over these a few times more until you can repeat them by heart. And then I think you had best be going. Your family will be looking for you."

Elizabeth bent over the faded words, saying them aloud as the doctor pointed to each with an old quill pen. She scarcely heard the houseman chopping wood for the breakfast fire or smelled the fragrance of bacon sizzling. Only the appearance of Madge, red-eyed and tearful, brought her back to reality. By then she was ready.

All the way to the house she recited the words under her breath. And when she reached the dining room where the family, silent and heavy of spirit, was gathering around the table, she placed herself in front of her father.

"I meant it when I promised to be like a son to you," she said. "I have begun to study Greek, and I can already recite the Greek article." Rapidly she began, "*Hoe, hee, toe* . . ."

All at once she faltered. She was trying to please Father. Why was he turning away and drawing a fresh handkerchief from his pocket?

Then Mother was saying in a tremulous voice, "Sit down, Elizabeth, and eat your porridge."

Confused, Elizabeth took her place. Was there no one who was pleased that she had mastered the difficult Greek lesson? No one who approved of her decision to be all that Eleazer had been?

3

NOT GO TO COLLEGE?

*N*ow, gentlemen, and Miss Cady, if you will give me your attention, I should like to make an announcement." The schoolmaster folded his arms on his desk and waited for his pupils to put away their pens and ink.

Outside the autumn wind whirled dry leaves through the crisp air. Elizabeth, now fourteen, was beginning her third year in the Latin, Greek, and higher mathematics classes usually limited to male students at the Johnstown Academy, a private coeducational boarding and day school of high caliber, which attracted pupils from an extensive area.

Elizabeth had first learned to read and cipher at Miss Maria Yost's dame school, then had been enrolled in the Academy, which was conveniently located on hilly Market Street a short distance above the Cady home. She had quickly advanced to the head of her grade, maintaining that position year after year.

After a year of Greek under Dr. Hosack's tutelage, Elizabeth, at Daniel Cady's request, had been permitted by the Academy authorities to enroll as a special student in the advanced classes for young men studying in preparation for college. What a thrilling moment that had been! Surely Father's arranging for her to be educated as Eleazer had been was proof that he thought she was filling Eleazer's place.

That she was the youngest member of the class and the only girl did not daunt her. The boys, however, kept her aware of her unique position. If she sat quietly and said nothing, one would remark, just loudly enough for her to hear, "It was a mistake to let a girl in our class. The poor ninny can't think of a thing to say." When she recited, she must be very sure that she was correct. Otherwise the boys would say, "There's that stupid girl making a mistake again." Elizabeth imagined that every time she opened her mouth not only she but every girl in the world was being judged by what she said.

The master was rapping on his desk with a ruler. "It is my pleasure to announce," he said, "that again this year there will be two prizes awarded for excellence in Greek. I need not remind you of the honor to the recipients. Not only will each one receive a visible token of his achievement, but the distinction will be noted on his scholastic record, thereby advancing the possibility of his admission to college." He paused a moment. "In fact, the winning of such a prize will undoubtedly assure enrollment in Union College."

The teacher's words rang clarion clear in Elizabeth's ears. If she were to win a Greek prize, how pleased Father would be! Even Eleazer had not succeeded in gaining such an honor. Yes, she would set her sights on a Greek prize. The next step would then be Union College. The master had said so. There was no telling what she might do after that. She might even become a second Portia.

Her common sense warned that such an idea was utter folly. Elizabeth had never heard of a woman lawyer, just as she had never heard of a woman doctor, preacher, or banker. Women did not enter business or the professions, but remained in their own or relatives' homes, dependent for their livelihood upon fathers, husbands, brothers, or sons. If there

were no men in their lives, and they must somehow earn a
living, they became seamstresses or school teachers. Even in
those fields men had the advantage, for a tailor commanded
higher prices than a dressmaker, and a male teacher usually
earned twice the salary paid a woman.

In high hopes Elizabeth studied her Greek lessons. And
night after night she dreamed of winning one of the prizes.
Always the ending of her dream was the same. Father in a
joyful voice exclaimed, "Elizabeth, my dear, you are as capable as a boy. Why should I long for a son when I have
you?"

Not all Elizabeth's time outside the Academy was devoted to study. Nearly every day she rode out on her chestnut mare over the Johnstown hills, for she had mastered the
difficult sidesaddle and cumbersome riding habit. Sometimes
she was accompanied by Peter, exercising her father's favorite stallion. At other times one of the law students might go
with her. Often she rode to nearby Fonda to watch the
colorful canal boats slowly drawn by horses or mules along
the newly built Erie Canal.

Frequently Dr. Hosack invited her to go with him in his
light carriage when he visited members of his congregation
who lived in the country, and permitted her to take the
reins. As they drove along leafy lanes or between plowed
fields, he would quiz her on the classics or discuss points of
philosophy.

In November Elizabeth celebrated her fifteenth birthday
with her first grown-up party, an elegant evening affair with
music, dancing, and elaborate refreshments. From then on
she was allowed to take part in many of the social activities
planned by Tryphena and her husband, Edward Bayard,

once a friend and classmate of Eleazer's, and now a law student in Father's office. The young couple lived in the spacious Cady home, and arranged frequent parties, picnics, and excursions—nutting expeditions in the autumn, skating and sleighing outings in the winter, and long walks in the spring looking for wildflowers.

How wonderful it was, after the crushing gloom of Eleazer's death, to play on the new piano, and to sing the new songs that Edward bought. Even more thrilling were the books he ordered—romances such as Sir Walter Scott's *Waverly, Guy Mannering,* or *Ivanhoe,* or the novel set in her own New York State, *The Last of the Mohicans* by James Fenimore Cooper. Elizabeth thought she could never be grateful enough to dear Edward. Home had become a more pleasant, cheerful place since he had joined the family.

There were frequently visits from friends and relatives, chiefly Mother's kin, the Livingstons of noble Scottish descent, who held vast estates and important positions in New York State.

Three times a year, in October, February, and May, court was held at the County Courthouse in Johnstown. School was dismissed and many businesses closed down, for court week was like a holiday. Elizabeth rarely missed a session. Accompanied sometimes by Madge and always by Peter, she sat for hours in the old courthouse, where the floor was covered four inches deep in sawdust into which people threw peach pits, peanut shells, and apple cores, or squirted streams of thick, brown tobacco juice. When the judge marched to his high bench, the constables pounded their long poles on the floor for attention.

The most exciting part of each session for Elizabeth was

when Father rose to speak. It was thrilling to hear him present the points of a case, one by one, with methodical precision. Often he kept the most important for the last, confounding his opponents with an unexpected witness or piece of evidence, and eliciting a burst of laughter or applause from the spectators.

In the evenings Elizabeth often followed Father into his office, sometimes taking her lessons along to study while he pored over his law cases. Sometimes she asked him to explain the parts of trials that puzzled her.

Through the bitter winter cold Elizabeth trudged daily over icy walks to the Academy, while sleighs slid past, their horses' bells jingling and runners squeaking.

During the spring she kept at her studies while Johnstown throbbed with westward-moving traffic: freight wagons filled with household goods; and farm carts piled high, with a cow tied to the back, followed by a string of barefoot children driving a few pigs or sheep. It seemed as if all the world were moving out to western New York, Ohio, Indiana, or beyond.

Finally came the last day of school and the long-awaited presentation of prizes. For Elizabeth only two mattered, those for excellence in Greek.

Viewing herself in the hall mirror at noontime, Elizabeth decided that her new gown in a heavenly shade of blue did indeed bring out the color of her eyes and heighten her clear complexion, as Madge had said. If only she were tall and slender like Madge instead of barely five feet and verging on plumpness.

At luncheon Elizabeth was almost too excited to eat. Her marks were very high, she knew. Only one other student,

Thurgood Ward, had as fine a record. She was almost sure that she would win one of the Greek prizes. But serious doubts assailed her. A week ago she had hesitated over the translation of a phrase. And only yesterday she had misspelled a word. Would those faults affect her nearly perfect record?

As the meal drew to a close, Father slid his napkin into its ring and looked at his watch. "If you will excuse me," he said to his wife, "I must return to my office. A client is coming within a few minutes, and I wish to look over some papers beforehand."

"Won't you be at the prize-giving?" Elizabeth asked.

"Not this year. I have attended it often in the past. One such occasion is much like another."

"But this year—" Elizabeth began.

"This year—what?" Father asked impatiently.

Elizabeth swallowed. What guarantee had she that she would win a prize? None. Better not to hint at the possibility than to disappoint Father.

"This year it may be different," she finished lamely.

Father turned to leave. "If it is, you must tell me about it," he said from the doorway. "My client will not remain long. I shall be free later in the afternoon."

Beneath the table's edge, Elizabeth frantically wrung her hands. To be so near her cherished dream—and yet not to be sure of its outcome! What would the next two hours bring?

How she sat through the first part of the program she never knew. Johnstown Academy was crowded to capacity with an eager audience. Automatically Elizabeth joined her class in singing verses of the national anthem, her eyes fixed on the flag with its twenty-five stars. Like an automaton she applauded when honors were awarded in penmanship, composition, and arithmetic to students in the lower grades.

Then the classics master walked importantly to the platform. In his hand he carried two slim, leather-bound volumes which he laid impressively on the lectern.

"It is my privilege to award the prizes for excellence in the study of Greek," he began. "I am sure that you are all aware of the hours of study, the stretching of the intellect, and the strain of competition for the students involved."

There were nods of approval in the audience. Elizabeth held her breath. The suspense was agonizing.

"The first prize goes to Thurgood Ward."

The words fell upon Elizabeth's ears with a sound of doom. So Thurgood had won, after all. She watched the young man rise and march to the platform, his face brick red. The audience applauded.

The master held up his hand for silence, and Elizabeth's heart began to flutter. Was there still a chance she might win a prize?

"Before announcing the recipient of the second prize, I should like to say that this year of 1830 marks a break with tradition in the history of Johnstown Academy. But the student in question has been so outstanding a scholar that there was no doubt in my mind or the minds of the other faculty members as to the justice of our decision."

The master paused. In the silence Elizabeth could feel the throbbing of her pulse.

Then the teacher cleared his throat, raised his chin, and said, "It is my pleasure to announce that the second prize for excellence in Greek goes to Elizabeth Smith Cady."

Hardly knowing whether her feet were touching the floor, Elizabeth made her way to the platform. She was buoyed up by a tremendous sense of achievement. She had proved that a girl could learn Greek, and that she could learn it better than most of the boys in the class. She could hardly wait to tell Father.

As her fingers closed upon the New Testament in Greek, she remembered to thank the master. She longed to run out the door and down the hill to Father's office. But she must behave properly and remain until the program was over.

At last the strains of "America" signified the end of the exercises. Elizabeth smiled and bowed her way through congratulating friends. If only they would not detain her!

Then she was out the door and flying down Market Street, her hat blowing back from her hair, her long skirts billowing. No carriage stood in front of the house; Father's client must have left. Out of breath, she pushed open the door, and burst into the office.

Father sat at his desk, just as in her dream. "Was the program different this year?" he asked.

"This year, for the first time, the second Greek prize was awarded to a girl, Father!" Then she could contain her excitement no longer. "I won it! I won it! The Greek prize is mine! Look, here it is!" She held out the New Testament.

Impatiently she waited, watching for the expected gleam of joy, listening for the anticipated words. Her heart was pounding. Why was Father so slow to speak? Was it because he was searching for an accolade appropriate to so outstanding an accomplishment?

While she stood there, hardly daring to breathe, he turned the volume over and over in his hands, examining it. At last he looked up, smiled sadly, and gave a deep sigh. "Oh, my gifted daughter," he said mournfully, "if only you had been born a boy!"

For a few seconds Elizabeth stared at him in disbelief, the fragments of her shattered dream cutting into her heart. Not a word of praise from Father, not a hint of pride that *his* daughter was the first ever to win the Greek prize! All her work, all her striving had not convinced him that a daughter's worth was equal to a son's.

Elizabeth ran from the room, fled to the garden, and sobbed out her disappointment and despair to Dr. Hosack.

A week later she had regained her balance. She must not blame Father for reacting as he had. He was still grieving for Eleazer, she knew. She could see the sorrow in his face every time he spoke to one of the young men in his office. If you were but my son, his eyes said.

The only thing for her to do, thought Elizabeth, was to continue with her education as if nothing had happened. Of course, most young women had no opportunity for book learning beyond that given in academies—and very few had that. Most girls were lucky if they learned to read and write while helping their mothers with the never-ending household tasks and looking after younger brothers and sisters. As soon as they reached marriageable age, they must begin to care for homes of their own and, not long after, a brood of children. Many people believed that the development of the intellect was unsettling to the feminine mind. Elizabeth had heard tales of women who had become insane from too much reading. What a ridiculous idea! She was thankful her parents were not of that opinion.

As the summer deepened, Elizabeth decided it was time

for her to begin preparations for going away to college. When Eleazer had gone, the whole household had been busy sewing on buttons, counting shirts, or helping to pack.

One noon at the dinner table, she said, "I have been wondering what clothes I should take with me to Schenectady in the fall. Do you think, Mother, that I shall need a ball gown?"

"To Schenectady? Have you been invited to visit someone there?"

"No, Mother. I mean when I go there to college."

Tryphena gave an audible sniff. Edward looked up with a piercing glance. Mrs. Cady's fork clattered to her plate.

"What do you mean—college?" she asked.

"Union College, of course," Elizabeth replied. "That's where Eleazer went, and I want to go also." She looked toward her father, confident of his approval.

To her consternation, Father was frowning. "Surely you must know that *you* cannot go to college," he stated in his most judicial voice.

"I can't see why not," Elizabeth said. "The boys go. Why can't I as well? I know I could do the work."

"It's not a question of your ability. It's because there isn't a college in the land that will admit women."

"That rule is for other people, not me," Elizabeth said indignantly. "Have you forgotten, Father, that I won the Greek prize? When the master first announced it, he said that the winner could gain admission to any college in the country!" Out of the corner of her eye she caught Edward's startled nod of agreement.

"He did not mean to include you, my dear," Father said. "He was addressing his male pupils."

Elizabeth could feel the blood rising to her head. Striving to keep her voice calm, she said, "Male or female—what difference should it make when it's a question of learning? I've proved that my mind is as good as a boy's."

"But there are rules barring women from colleges," Daniel Cady stated.

"There were rules keeping girls out of the boys' classes at the Academy, but you made it possible for me to be enrolled. You could do the same at Union College. I'm sure of it."

"And I am far from sure that the college authorities would admit you, no matter how hard I urged them. Such a thing has never been done," Daniel Cady said sternly.

Elizabeth clasped her hands tightly together, her eyes riveted on her father. He was the most powerful individual in Johnstown. Everyone looked up to him. Everyone asked his advice and followed his decisions without question. There was no one more influential in all the county, she was sure.

"Please, Father! Promise that you'll ask Union College to let me in."

Daniel Cady pursed his lips in the tight line she knew so well. That was the way he looked when he had to impart unwelcome information to his clients, especially women.

"Such a step would be entirely without precedent," he said coldly. "I cannot see that anything I might say would change the situation."

Close to tears, Elizabeth begged, "But you will try, won't you, Father?"

Tryphena tossed her head. "You should be thankful that Father interceded for you at the Academy, Lizzie. You must not ask him to make himself ridiculous by this silly request."

"Silly!" Elizabeth exploded. "I was never more serious in my life."

"Many people would consider it foolish," Tryphena contended. "We would not want you to be a laughingstock. No one has ever heard of a girl going to college. And what good would it do?"

"At least I'd learn as much as some of the law students," Elizabeth stated in fury. "Then I wouldn't have to feel so stupid when they tell me how much more they know than I do." She caught Edward's eye on her, and added, "Not you, Edward, of course."

Mrs. Cady sighed. "There's more to life than book learning," she said, "but there are times when I wish . . ." Her voice trailed off as her husband cleared his throat for attention.

"If you can learn to manage a household and care for your husband, children, and servants as capably as your mother does, you'll be filling your place in the universe, Elizabeth," Daniel Cady pronounced pontifically.

Her place in the universe! Elizabeth thought in rebellion. Was she to spend her life bearing children, planning meals, and tending to the needs of others? Of what use, then, were all her efforts to excel in her studies? What she really wanted was to—to—

Her thoughts jolted to a halt. What did she really want? Of only one fact was she certain. She did not want to be trapped within the narrow confines of the average woman's lot.

But what was she to do? Most avenues were barred to her. If she had been a boy she would have been well on her way to becoming a lawyer, going first to college, then accompanying Father to courtroom and state house. As a girl she had no profession to aim for or occupation to take up except schoolteaching or dressmaking. And she wished to do neither.

Even if she were burning with a desire to work, she would meet family opposition. Daniel Cady was a wealthy man, proud of his position in Johnstown and New York. He would be hurt if people assumed that he was unable to support his daughter. There was another point, too. She could almost hear him arguing that if she were to work, she would be keeping wages from some needy person.

Elizabeth gritted her teeth. The whole situation was impossible. Because women were barred from professions requiring further education—the law, ministry, and medicine—they were denied the education and training for those professions. As a consequence they were denied all opportunities for higher learning. She felt as if she were at the bottom of a pit of prejudice and ignorance.

So deep in thought was she that she scarcely heard her mother's voice.

"Elizabeth, how would you like to make a visit to Peterboro?"

Elizabeth was jerked back to reality. Peterboro! The home of Cousin Gerrit Smith and his lovely wife Nancy and their daughter, another Elizabeth, to whom she felt even closer than her own sisters. That they had both been named after Grandmother Elizabeth Livingston gave them a special bond.

Normally the prospect would have filled Elizabeth with pure joy. Today she was so numb with disappointment at not going to college that she could hardly take in the idea.

Dazedly she heard her father's voice, raised in rare irascibility. "Why do you want to expose Elizabeth to Gerrit and all his radical ideas?" he demanded. "You know she'll come home with her head stuffed full of his liberal nonsense."

Suddenly Elizabeth was all attention. She had never known Father to speak in such a way, especially of Cousin Gerrit, one of the wealthiest landowners in the state. He could live like a king if he chose. But instead he kept his home, spacious though it was, so simple and unostentatious that even the humblest of his many guests felt comfortable there.

Elizabeth watched her mother draw herself up proudly. She's like a queen, thought Elizabeth.

"Gerrit is one of my dearest relatives," Mother said in an icy tone Elizabeth had never heard her use to Father. "His entire life is given over to the service of those less fortunate than he. I am confident that any ideas Elizabeth may gain in his home will be of the highest nature."

"Do you consider the flouting of the law a laudable thing?" Daniel Cady demanded. "You are aware, no doubt, that Gerrit is rumored to harbor runaway slaves on his estate."

Mother's gaze darkened. "Poor wretches," she murmured.

"Surely you cannot be in sympathy with *abolitionists?*" Father asked. "They are fanatics, stirring up strife and undermining our legal system."

Elizabeth listened in shocked silence. Never before had she heard her parents argue—at least, not in the presence of other family members. She had heard murmurs from their bedroom from time to time, when Mother's chill voice could mean only disapproval of Father's views. Today was the first time she had witnessed an open difference of opinion.

Just then the housemaid appeared. "Excuse me, Mr. Cady, sir, but a gentleman has come to see you who says it's very urgent."

Daniel Cady threw his rumpled napkin on the table. That action alone was indicative of his disturbed state of mind. He left in unwonted haste, without apology or request for leave to be excused. His departure was so unlike his usual courteous withdrawal when called from the table that the family sat for a few moments in silence.

Elizabeth was the first to speak. "I'd like very much to go to Peterboro," she said. "When may I leave?"

4

LEGALLY RIGHT BUT MORALLY WRONG

*I*n mounting excitement Elizabeth stared out the open window of the stage. Each landmark quickened her expectation. In a short time she would reach the crossroads where she would be met by Cousin Gerrit's coachman.

Thank goodness she had the seat next to the window and could look out. She was thankful, too, that the day was fair. If it were raining, the leather curtains would be fastened, and the interior of the coach would be as dank and shadowy as a cave. She longed to be outside with the driver, but she had promised Mother to be ladylike on this, her first unescorted journey. It had been planned that Hattie would accompany her, but at the last minute a letter had come from young Daniel Eaton that had thrown Hattie into a frenzy of excitement. Daniel was coming up from New York City; she had to be in Johnstown when he arrived. He might even be going to ask Father for her hand.

After many admonitions as to correct conduct, Elizabeth had been permitted to travel alone. No proper young lady rode outside with the coach driver. So here she was, penned up with these dull, older people who could talk of nothing but the discomfort of the trip.

Beside her a stout woman whined, "Land sakes, if this dust ain't the worst I've ever known. It gets right into a body's lungs."

A spare man with a weather-beaten countenance said in a rasping voice, "This ain't nothin' to what I've seed in the Ohio country. You take a train of settlers' wagons with all their sheep and cattle, and they kick up a real cloud. I've et dust for a week out West."

She need not listen to them, Elizabeth thought. Instead she could mull over what had been uppermost in her thoughts since Mother had asked if she would like to visit the Smiths.

Abolition was a subject that was rarely mentioned at home, and never discussed. Now she could understand why. Mother's few words had indicated her feeling on the matter. And as usual, Father was adamant in his adherence to the law. One question was bothering Elizabeth. Which of her parents was in the right?

She knew that Mother had a deep compassion for all people. The servants had orders never to turn a tramp away hungry. Baskets of food and clothing went out regularly from the Cady house to poor homes. And Mother often listened patiently to poverty-stricken ladies' woeful recitals, as she poured out cup after cup of tea for unhappy callers.

Of course Mother would feel sorry for runaway slaves. But was it right to help them? They were, Father said, the legal property of their masters, just as Penny, her horse, was Elizabeth's property. If Penny should run off, Elizabeth would expect someone to bring her back. The Southern slaveholder had paid good money for his slaves. Had he not the right to expect that they be returned to him?

If Cousin Gerrit did indeed harbor fugitives from slavery, would Elizabeth see any of them? In her mind's eye she pictured a dusky, brutish figure crouched in a shadowy corner of the barn at Peterboro.

A heavy jolt almost bounced Elizabeth off the worn leather seat. Ahead she could see the spire of a church. They were almost at the crossroads. She wiped her face with her handkerchief, and flicked the dust from her blue traveling dress.

Ah, there was a carriage, and jumping down from it, her full skirts billowing, was a young girl. Libby had come to meet her! Joyfully Elizabeth waved from the window.

Minutes later she was seated in the carriage beside her cousin. The coachman had piled her trunks on the rack, and was urging the perfectly matched bays ahead. The light vehicle started up smoothly, and was soon bowling along the country road in shade cast by overhanging trees. A cool breeze fanned Elizabeth's cheeks. She swept off her bonnet to let the wind blow through her curls. What a delight to travel so swiftly and easily after hours in the lumbering coach!

The two girls chatted feverishly, often interrupting each other as they exchanged news of their families.

Soon the carriage was rolling up a long drive between stately elms, broad green lawns, and colorful flower beds to a large square house with tall pillars. On the porch stood Cousin Gerrit, a smile of welcome on his face.

Moments later Elizabeth felt the clasp of his arms about her, and caught a whiff of cologne from the handkerchief in his breast pocket. Then he was holding her off at arm's length.

"I declare, Elizabeth, you grow more attractive with

every passing month. And I hear that you have earned a special honor. It's not every day that we can welcome to Peterboro a young woman who has earned a prize for excellence in Greek!"

Elizabeth felt a glow of pure happiness. Cousin Gerrit always knew what would give the most pleasure to others.

Then Cousin Nancy was approaching, looking like a goddess, her auburn hair coiled smoothly, her pale-green gown faultless. She touched her cool cheek to Elizabeth's. "How good to see you, my dear," she said.

"Come on up and change, or we'll be late for dinner," Libby urged. Elizabeth fairly floated up the broad staircase.

An hour later Elizabeth counted thirty people at the long table. A sandy-haired itinerant preacher, a rotund lawyer and his rosy wife, a merchant from Philadelphia, two weary-looking women schoolteachers, a jolly bewhiskered peddler, and a young couple on their way West were among the guests. Far down the table were two copper-hued faces. Cousin Gerrit always invited his Indian friends to share his food.

And what a bountiful meal it was! The host carved a magnificent haunch of beef, while servants brought in dishes heaped with peas, beans, beets, and carrots from the garden. There were ears of fresh corn to be buttered and eaten from the cob, and platters of biscuits made from the recipe Cousin Nancy had brought from her Maryland home.

As he cut slices of succulent beef, Cousin Gerrit remarked, "I wonder if we should not become vegetarians. I have just read an article which claims that the killing of God's creatures is incompatible with a life of nonviolence."

While the pros and cons of various diets were discussed,

Elizabeth gave an inward sigh. She could hardly wait for her plate to be filled, and hoped the Smiths would not immediately forego the eating of meat.

A few minutes later the lawyer's wife asked Nancy, "Have you seen the new fashions from Paris?"

"I have, and I think those tightly laced waists and sweeping skirts are dangerous!" Cousin Gerrit interrupted. "How can any woman take a deep breath with her lungs compressed in such a ridiculous manner? Or walk upstairs without tripping? I hope that I never see any of my family tricked out in such unhealthful outfits!"

Elizabeth and Libby, who had secretly admired the new styles, exchanged covert glances.

A moment later the preacher asked the lawyer, "Have you seen the new prison at Ossining?"

"I have, and it's a sight I don't wish to see again soon," the attorney replied. "The men are made to work together in complete silence. If they speak a word, or lift their eyes from their work, they are flogged mercilessly."

"Perhaps Philadelphia has a better idea in putting all its prisoners into solitary confinement so that they may repent of their sins. The prison is called a penitentiary for that reason," offered the preacher.

"There must be some better means to teach men the error of their ways," Gerrit commented. "Our system of punishment is all wrong, especially the death penalty. When will we learn that we cannot wipe out sin by destroying life?"

The arrival of dessert—mounds of crimson raspberries, bowls of creamy custards, and thin slices of golden pound cake—soon occupied the diners' attention. When all had finished, Cousin Nancy rose.

Some of the gentlemen stood by their chairs, and one looked expectantly at the goblet he had just drained of water.

"I trust you are not expecting brandy and cigars after dinner," Cousin Gerrit remarked. "We keep a temperance house here. I look upon spiritous liquors as a source of evil rather than pleasure. And tobacco I consider a noxious weed injurious to the lungs."

The gentleman hid his discomfiture, but poorly. Elizabeth, however, felt a glow of pride. Not many men had the courage to stand up against established custom. Into her mind flashed the memory of the bruise on Flora Campbell's cheek, and Cook's explanation of why Billy had been born without arms.

In the spacious drawing room the talk went on and on, until Elizabeth's head was fairly bursting with the effort of trying to remember new names and places. She had thought that her parents and their friends were well informed. She tried to keep up with the news in the daily papers. But here at Peterboro she felt like a stranger in another world.

Cousin Nancy was asking a gentleman who sat nearby, "What is the latest news from Philadelphia?"

"Young Mr. Garrison will arrive soon to give a series of lectures. He will stay with James and Lucretia Mott," the man replied.

Cousin Gerrit leaned forward. "The cause of emancipation will advance rapidly in the company of those three," he said.

Who was Mr. Garrison? Elizabeth wondered. And the Motts?

As if in answer to her unspoken query, Nancy remarked to Gerrit, "Some of our guests may not know of whom we speak."

"William Lloyd Garrison is a young writer from Massachusetts who believes in the immediate emancipation of slaves," Gerrit explained. "In Baltimore he was clapped into jail for writing an article attacking a Newburyport sea captain who transported slaves from Baltimore to New Orleans. It is good news that he has been released and will speak in Philadelphia. The Motts are leaders in the antislavery movement there. Mrs. Mott is an extremely eloquent preacher against slavery."

Elizabeth listened, her head spinning. Slavery was lawful in the southern states, she knew. Had Mr. Garrison a right to attack a situation that had legal sanction? She was amazed that Cousin Gerrit would speak so approvingly of a man who defied the law. Surprising, too, was his last remark. A woman preacher? It was unheard of for a woman to speak in public. Elizabeth could hardly believe her ears.

"I heard today of a fugitive slave that was caught in Oriskany Falls," the peddler offered. "His owner had chased him all the way from Georgia. They say the poor Negro wept when he was led away."

"I don't see how his master had the heart," one of the teachers observed.

"Of course he had the *legal* right to claim his property," Elizabeth said.

There was an instant's silence. She could feel many eyes upon her. Then Cousin Gerrit said gently, "Sometimes a thing may be legally right but morally wrong."

The words struck through Elizabeth's mind like an arrow, crystallizing the thought she had tried to express long ago in Father's office.

"When a law is not right, people should work to change it," she declared, hearing in her inner ear her father's voice.

"And until the law is changed," Cousin Gerrit asked softly, "what should one do, Elizabeth?"

The memory of her father's words was strong upon her. "Obey the old law, of course," she said.

As if a shade had been pulled down over his face, Gerrit's expression changed. The eyes were still a clear gray, the brows neatly defined above them, and the thin mouth curved in a pleasant smile. But the light that had sparkled in his eyes was gone, the tenderness from his lips. "It is natural for us to cling to the precepts of our childhood," he said.

Throughout the evening Elizabeth felt Cousin Gerrit's gaze returning to rest upon her. It was almost a relief when the local guests began to leave, and those remaining overnight started for their rooms.

When Elizabeth approached the hall table where the bedtime candlesticks stood in a row, Cousin Gerrit drew near and spoke in a tone so soft that only she could hear.

"Come with me, Elizabeth. There is someone I want you to meet."

Another introduction at this hour when she was half asleep and could remember the names of only a few of the guests she had met earlier?

"Couldn't we wait until tomorrow?" she asked.

"I'm afraid not."

She turned to go back into the drawing room, but Gerrit put a lighted taper in her hand.

"This way, if you please," he said, and started up the stairs.

Dutifully she followed him up one flight, then another, to the third floor. He stooped to insert a key in a solid wooden door, unlocked it, and entered.

"It's all right, Harriet," he said softly. "Do not be afraid."

Elizabeth followed him into the room. Into the circle of light formed by their two candles glided a figure, slender and graceful, clad in gray. Gerrit held his candle toward the young woman, lighting a face of singular beauty framed by dark, wavy hair, the lips trembling and the eyes dilated with fear.

"Elizabeth, I want you to meet another guest. Her name is Harriet. She escaped yesterday from her master, who is visiting in Syracuse. Later tonight she will start for Canada, disguised as a Quakeress. You may never again have the opportunity of seeing a slave girl face to face, so ask her all you wish to know about slavery. I shall leave you together while I make preparations for her departure." He handed the key to Elizabeth. "Lock the door, and open to no one but me." Then he was gone.

Elizabeth looked at the girl. She could be no more than a year or two older than herself. And her skin was a pale olive.

"How can you be a slave when you don't look the least bit like a Negress?" Elizabeth asked.

"That is because I am a quadroon. One quarter of the blood in my veins is black."

"One quarter?" Elizabeth asked.

"My mother was the daughter of a black slave and a white man. My father was white, also."

"Is he your master?"

"No. He sold me when I was fourteen to another man —the one I ran away from."

Elizabeth gasped. "Your own father sold you!" she exclaimed.

The girl shrugged wordlessly.

"Why did you run away?" Elizabeth asked as soon as she could speak. "Was your master unkind to you?"

"I did not like him," Harriet said shortly.

"Why?" demanded Elizabeth. "Did he beat you?"

The girl shrugged her shoulders. "Not often. Only when he was cross with me."

Elizabeth looked at the girl's slender hands, the fingers as soft as her own. Obviously the girl had not worked in the fields, and she showed no signs of having been mistreated.

"You must have had a good reason for running away," she persisted.

"When my mistress was sickly—and she was sickly most of the time—my master made me lie with him."

Elizabeth drew back at the bluntness of the words. She could not look at the young woman.

"I had a baby by him," Harriet continued. "It was a girl, born dead. I thanked God for saving it from a life like mine."

Elizabeth stood in stunned silence. To come face to face with someone who had been subjected to such degradation was like a shock of icy water.

Just then there came a gentle tap on the door, and Gerrit's voice saying, "Elizabeth, you may unlock the door."

As her cousin entered the room, Elizabeth turned to Harriet. Now Elizabeth was the one who was trembling. How could I ever have been so blind, she thought, as to think a slave was property? Merely because lawmakers in southern states declared the system legal?

Suddenly nothing mattered except that Harriet reach Canada and freedom. Elizabeth clasped her hands together. "Tell me," she said, "how I can help you. Surely there must be something I can do."

Harriet stood silent. Gerrit answered for her. "You can keep what you have seen here tonight an absolute secret. Now I must take Harriet downstairs and out to the carriage. One of my clerks is going with her to Oswego and will take her by boat across Lake Ontario to Canada. Will you be good enough to go ahead and see if the way is clear?"

Elizabeth crept softly down the stairs, almost as fearful as if she herself were the one whose freedom was in peril. The halls were empty and silent. At the great front door she waited while two shadows moved soundlessly down the staircase and out into the night.

A muffled figure waited in the carriage. Cousin Gerrit caught up a warm cloak, held it for Harriet, and helped her into the vehicle with as much care as if she had been a fine lady. When it had wheeled out of sight, he came back into the house.

For a moment Elizabeth looked at him, her candle sputtering between them.

"Now do you think it right to uphold a law that would return slaves to their masters?" he asked.

Elizabeth brushed back tears.

"You do not need to speak, my dear," Gerrit said. "I knew your heart would tell you that God's law is above any that man may make."

Elizabeth slept badly, tortured by dreams of Harriet's capture. The next day she was horrified to see a faultlessly attired gentleman on a magnificent horse ride up to the house, accompanied by two marshals from Syracuse. In an agony of fear she heard Gerrit invite them to make a search of the house and outbuildings. In mounting nervousness she learned that the visitors had been invited for dinner. How she sat through the meal she never knew. Each time she was engaged in conversation she replied shortly or not at all, so fearful was she that some chance slip might give away her secret.

The sun was sinking low when the travelers departed. Even then Elizabeth's mind was not at rest. Suppose they should catch up with Harriet and her companion?

The next two days seemed interminable. Toward nightfall a dusty clerk arrived and went with Gerrit into his study. A few minutes later he called Elizabeth into the room.

"Harriet is safe in Canada," he said.

Elizabeth stole off to a quiet corner of the garden, filled with thankfulness. At the same time she was tortured by contrition. How had she ever been so heartless as to think it right that fugitive slaves be remanded to servitude?

Suddenly she came to attention. Was it only a few days ago that she had accepted without question Father's statement that runaway slaves were property and should be returned to their legal owners? After meeting Harriet, Elizabeth knew that such action, however lawful, was cruel and heartless. She would rather have died than betray Harriet!

From earliest childhood Elizabeth had considered Father the ultimate authority on any and all matters. It was shattering to realize that his judgment was not always faultless.

Long ago, as a little girl, she had learned that the law, especially in regard to women, was not invariably fair. Now she was discovering that Father himself, until this moment a very pillar of justice and equity in her eyes, was not always right.

Despite the warmth of the summer air, Elizabeth shivered. If she could not put her trust in the law and her father, where should she turn?

Slowly the realization came that in some matters she could not accept the opinions of other persons, however wise and experienced they might be. She and only she could decide what to her was right or wrong. From now on she would have to think through such problems for herself.

5

AMERICA'S MOST MODERN
SCHOOL FOR GIRLS

*W*hether her father attempted to use his influence to win her acceptance at Union College Elizabeth never knew. Upon her return home she learned that she was to attend Mrs. Emma Willard's Troy Female Seminary. It would be more of a Female Cemetery, Elizabeth thought unhappily, although it was a pioneer establishment of sound learning for young women and was considered the best such institution in the country. What a change to go from the academy where there had been only boys in her classes to a school in which there would be only girls! To be far away from home and all her friends, shut up with a hundred other girl boarders, with two hundred more girls as day pupils—the prospect was unbearable.

Heavy of heart, Elizabeth set out for Troy in 1830. Soon, however, her natural buoyancy returned, for the journey was an adventure in itself. Instead of going all the way by stage, she traveled on the newly opened Mohawk and Hudson River Railroad from Schenectady to Albany.

From her seat in the former stagecoach fitted with flange wheels, she could look ahead at the puffing, snorting little locomotive called the *John Bull*. Its tall smokestack belched out smoke and sparks. Soon Elizabeth was brushing ashes and soot from her coat, and noted dark streaks on the other passengers' faces. Her own must be as dirty, she decided rue-fully.

At one point the train reached a hill too steep for the en-gine's limited power. A gentleman next to her explained that the passenger coaches would now be attached to a string of freight cars loaded with rocks on the other side of the hill. Soon the weight of the descending cars pulled the train up to the hill's summit. It passed down safely, and proceeded on its noisy way.

Perhaps the Seminary would not be as bad as she had feared, Elizabeth thought late in the afternoon as the stage from Albany drew up to a large four-story building opposite the courthouse on Second Street in Troy.

An older student met her at the door. "Come with me, and I'll show you to your room. The porter will bring your trunk up later." As they entered the hallway, she smiled at Elizabeth and asked, "Aren't you thankful to be here?"

"The train wasn't really dangerous," Elizabeth said.

"Oh, did you come by train? That must have been excit-ing. But I mean how privileged you must feel to be here as a student."

Elizabeth surveyed her wonderingly. "Privileged?"

"Of course. There are hundreds of girls who would give their right arms to have a chance at the education you'll be getting, but there just isn't room for them all."

The girl's hair was drawn back simply from her face and fastened in a neat coil. Her dress was of a plain cotton with-out ruffles or other trimming, gathered at the waist and fall-ing to her ankles, obviously made according to the school's specifications. She led the way down a long hall.

On one side Elizabeth glimpsed a large dining room where girls were busily setting out plates and cutlery. On the other side was a series of smaller rooms. From one came the notes of a piano.

Elizabeth followed her guide up a flight of broad stairs to the second floor, which contained a chapel, a reception room, and a tastefully furnished sitting room that appeared to be part of the principal's apartment.

Another flight of stairs took them to long rows of small bedrooms. Elizabeth paused at the landing, but her companion hurried upward.

"The new students all sleep on the fourth floor," she explained.

At last they stopped before an open door. "This will be your room," the girl said. "I'd better warn you now that you'll have to keep it neat at all times."

Elizabeth tossed her hat and gloves on the double bed and sank down upon it, noting that the tiny room also contained two straight wooden chairs, a bureau, and a small box stove.

The older student gasped in dismay. "You must *never* sit on the bed. And don't leave your things lying on it. Put them in the bureau, out of sight."

Elizabeth rose. "I suppose there are other rules?" she asked testily.

"Oh, yes. You and your roommate will each have full responsibility for your room for one week at a time. You will fill your water pitcher at the pump in the yard. And you can get coals for lighting your fire from a pan in the hall. There is a bell for rising at six-thirty, a bell for early morning study, for exercise, and for breakfast at eight. There are other bells all day long for classes and meals and outdoor exercise."

"It sounds terrible. You must hate those bells," Elizabeth said.

The girl looked at her disapprovingly. "It's a help to have them. Of course when I'm studying physiology I hate to be interrupted."

"Physiology?" Elizabeth asked. "Do you mean to say that the girls at this school are taught about the human body? How shocking—and exciting!"

"It's my favorite course," the girl stated. "But some parents made such a fuss that the teachers pasted heavy brown paper over all the pictures in our textbook so that we won't see anything to damage our morals."

Elizabeth gave her a searching glance. "Don't you ever peek?"

The girl looked uncomfortable. "Sometimes the paper comes unstuck," she admitted.

Suddenly a sharp clang sounded through the building. "That's the bell to mark the end of the exercise period," the guide said. "You'll just have time to tidy up before supper. You'd better hurry." Then she was gone.

Elizabeth opened a bureau drawer. It was filled with neatly folded piles of clothing. What a nuisance to have to share the bureau! She yanked open another drawer, found it bare, and thrust her hat and gloves inside. Then she poured water from the half-full pitcher into the large earthenware bowl and washed the dust from her hands and face. She was sure that she was going to hate this school with all its stupid restrictions. The only thing that sounded at all interesting was the class in physiology.

One warm July afternoon two years later, Elizabeth waited with other members of her class at the rear of the large hall where the annual public examination of the Troy Female Seminary pupils took place. An eight-day affair, the examination was one of the social events of Troy and Albany. Last year Elizabeth had been terrified by the ordeal. Today she could face it with some equanimity.

On the right side of the auditorium sat the spectators— prominent educators, clergymen, legislators, parents, and friends. Somewhere among them were her mother and father. Elizabeth stood on tiptoe, struggling for a glimpse of them. It was usually easy to locate Mother. Few women were as tall as she. Ah, there she was on the far side, in a new bonnet beribboned in lavender. And the smooth gray head beside hers was surely Father's.

There was a stir among the waiting girls as the leader gave a signal. One by one, dressed alike in simple white dresses with brightly colored sashes, they filed down the aisle and took their places on the left side of the hall, standing until the last girl had reached her chair, then all sat down at the same time.

Mrs. Willard advanced to the podium, tall and erect, robed in rich black satin with a white silk fichu. What a queenly figure she made, with her regal carriage and her classic features crowned by a white mull turban, Elizabeth thought.

Surely there was no woman in the world more to be admired than Mrs. Willard. When she had returned a year ago from her triumphal European tour, the whole school had welcomed her with reverence and love. For all her tremendous intelligence and international stature in the educational world, she took a keen personal interest in each pupil, giving scholarships to many with limited funds. Most of the girls adored her, and were determined to follow as closely as possible in her footsteps, becoming schoolteachers so that they might educate the next generation of girls in the advanced subjects they had learned.

The Troy Female Seminary boasted several advanced subjects, Elizabeth had discovered. In fact, some were dubbed unsuitable by critics. Why should young ladies learn about higher mathematics or geography? Little good it would do future housewives to know geometry or the boundaries of Switzerland. That Mrs. Willard had entered the field of authorship, writing textbooks on geography, was a dangerously radical step for a woman, too, they complained.

Mrs. Willard appeared undaunted by any criticism, and met it with skill and courage, as she was doing now. From the platform her voice sounded clearly throughout the hall. "Those gathered here today may wonder at the broad range of this school's curriculum, not equaled by any other girls' school in this country," she said. "The very pupils who excel most in those studies which men have been apt to think would unsex us, such as mathematics and natural philosophy, are the most apt to possess the elegant simplicity of fine manners."

That should silence some of the critics, thought Elizabeth, longing to clap her hands, but sitting straight and decorous, her fingers interlaced and ankles crossed.

"Even personal beauty is advanced," Mrs. Willard continued, "for as a woman improves in taste, and as her will gains efficiency in every species of self-control, she rarely fails to improve herself in symmetry of form."

And all the training at school helps, too, Elizabeth added silently, recalling the healthfully balanced program, the emphasis on cleanliness and good grooming.

"Genuine learning has ever been said to give polish to man," Mrs. Willard went on. "Why, then, should it not bestow added charms on woman?"

There was a scattering of applause.

Mrs. Willard then explained the examination procedure, after which the girls advanced to be questioned by their teachers. The geography class came first, each girl carrying her two-foot-square blackboard, on which she drew maps in colored chalk, and held aloft her work so that all might view it.

The class in logic was next examined. When Elizabeth recited she gave her replies in a clear voice, trying to make every word audible to the people in the back row. How she enjoyed stating the principles by which one arranged facts and ideas in order to proceed from one point to another in a reasonable sequence.

Natural philosophy, mathematics, and English composition followed, then the class in physiology. Elizabeth could feel the tension building up all around her. Would some of the mothers express their disapproval by leaving the room as they had the first time the subject had been discussed in public a few years ago?

"Please name the bones of the arm," a teacher requested.

Elizabeth could sense the other girls relaxing. No one could consider indelicate a reference to the arm.

"Kindly draw a diagram of the heart."

That, too, was above reproach. Evidently Mrs. Willard had decided to omit even the slightest reference to the human reproductive system, a subject certain to draw violent criticism.

"What elements are necessary to good health?"

Every girl in the school could reply to that, naming a wholesome diet, plenty of cold water, outdoor and indoor exercise, simple, unrestricting garments, regular mental occupation, and sufficient hours of sleep.

Such a program was advantageous, Elizabeth thought, looking at the rosy faces around her. Yes, the Troy Female Seminary had turned out to be much more enjoyable than she had at first imagined. She was even proud to be a "trudging Trojan," as the girls called themselves.

True, the constant bells at first made her nervous and irritable. But she soon learned that their clangor did not always signal study. Elizabeth had looked forward eagerly to the two hours of outdoor exercise at the end of the afternoon, even though it might be nothing more exciting than a walk in a long queue with other girls through Troy streets. Despite the constant presence of teacher chaperones, the girls often managed to exchange a glance or a whispered word with some of the young men students from nearby Rensselaer Polytechnic Institute, who invariably were afoot on the same route at that time of day. Of such attention Elizabeth had a generous share.

The regular hour of dancing after supper was fun, too. Elizabeth had learned to do the quadrille, reels, and even the controversial waltz, which some old fogies called the devil's greatest invention. She had, in fact, mastered the steps of

two—the lively Viennese and the slower Boston Waltz.
Of course at school there were only girls for partners, but in
Johnstown on holiday, or visiting at classmates' homes, there
were young men galore to dance with who were delighted
to find a partner who knew all the latest steps.

The music lessons, also, were a joy. Elizabeth liked to
sing, and learned to play accompaniment on the guitar.
Piano instruction was another pleasure, although the constant drill of scales and exercises was a bore. She would
much rather play lively airs like the "Russian March" or
"Napoleon Crossing the Rhine," and often did, as soon as
the rotund music master had closed the door of the practice
room.

As for studies, although Elizabeth had learned in the
Johnstown Academy as much Latin, Greek, and mathematics as were taught at Troy, she had found other subjects a
challenge.

The friendships with the girls were a delight. As Nancy
had predicted, Elizabeth had enjoyed visiting in other
homes, taking the elegant steamboat, the *Chief Justice Mar-
shall*, down the Hudson to New York City, or traveling
westward a distance on the Erie Canal.

What a variety of girls there were! Some were so studious
that they were dubbed "dulls." Others who had little interest beyond their few contacts with boys were termed
"flirts." And the fun-loving practical jokers were called
"romps."

Into each group Elizabeth had been welcomed. Her high
marks gave her entrée among the studious girls. Her popularity with boys and her wide range of masculine acquaint-
ances among family friends nearby made her sought after by

the flirts. And her mischievous pranks ensured her acceptance by the romps. Although undetected, she had created the greatest commotion of the year when late one night she kicked the official signal bell down a long flight of stairs. Its clangor roused students and faculty alike, and the resultant bedlam was remembered for years.

One of the features of the Seminary that Elizabeth liked especially were frequent opportunities to hear noted orators, often of international fame. She wished that she might have been a pupil when the great LaFayette himself had paid a visit to the school. She listened enthralled as a speaker reduced his listeners to tears, aroused them to fury, or moved them to laughter. How she would like to have such power!

The last girl finished her recitation, ending the examination period for the day. Mrs. Willard again approached the podium.

"Nothing can be more pleasing to the true friend of woman than the sight of a well-educated female bringing all her faculties into exercise in the performance of the appropriate duties of her sex, as mistress of a household, as a wife and mother. To prepare the rising generation of women for these important duties, and to bring forward teachers to aid me in this, has been the grand object of my life."

The assembled guests united in enthusiastic approval. Elizabeth looked toward her parents. Father would certainly think highly of such aims, she knew. So would every other man present, and many women.

But in Elizabeth's ears the words rang with a doleful sound. There were a hundred exciting things she longed to be—a lawyer, an orator, a newspaper editor, a legislator. Why must her choice be limited to wife or schoolteacher?

The applause died down, and Mrs. Willard continued. "I have noted," she said, "a widespread and disturbing tendency among women to devote themselves completely to the service of others. To my students here assembled I must say that it is questionable how far we have a right to sacrifice ourselves.

"God has given to each of his great family the care of one being, that is, of herself—and if she neglect this one, or inflict upon her unnecessary pain, or deny her reasonable gratifications, is she not unfaithful to her trust? To *have right*, as well as to *do right*, seems to be the duty of each individual."

Elizabeth noted each word. By the same argument she should have the right to decide what she would do with her life although she was hedged about by forces that denied her reasonable gratification in her choice of a career.

The problem was, where did her future lie? If only she might find a clear-cut pathway to follow, step by step, as she had the arguments in her logic class. Neither career suggested by Mrs. Willard really appealed to Elizabeth. For her the future loomed shadowy and uncertain, clouded by restrictions and frustrations.

Not even the congratulations of parents and friends could completely dispel her troubled thoughts.

6

WHAT OF THE FUTURE?

*O*f course the masculine mind is superior to the feminine," the young law student said with a complacence Elizabeth found infuriating. They stood on Main Street in Johnstown outside the Cady home one spring morning in 1839. The young man had just left Mr. Cady's office, and Elizabeth was about to enter the house after a brisk walk down to the river.

A newcomer to her father's office, this neophyte had the same conceit, the same feeling of male supremacy held by many aspiring lawyers, Elizabeth decided, and he apparently looked forward to proving his point in a discussion. He had probably heard from the other students that she was something of a crank on the place of woman, a real bluestocking. When they had met face to face for the first time he had seemed surprised at her appearance. She couldn't help but notice his admiration then, although she was used to such glances by now. Not that she was beautiful like Tryphena or Cousin Nancy, but men did seem to think her attractive. One had composed a poem about her "cheeks like a rose." And another had written his admiration of her "clustered ringlets." She did not dislike such compliments—what girl would?—but she treasured more a statement by Edward that he had never known a woman with a better mind. She must prove the truth of his belief.

Tilting back her head, she looked up into the law student's face. That she was shorter than he by at least a foot gave her a sense of inferiority. But she would not let him guess it and provide him with another weapon.

"On what premise do you base your opinion?" she inquired in her loftiest manner, thankful for her course in logic at Troy, and for the poise and self-assurance gained there.

"Take literature," he said. "Shakespeare proved the supremacy of man in *The Taming of the Shrew*. Don't you remember how Katharina gave in to Petruchio?"

Elizabeth remembered all too well Kate's sickening capitulation. She searched for another character. "What about Portia?" she countered in triumph. "She had the wit and intelligence to save Antonio's life."

The student smiled patronizingly. "Have you forgotten her speech to Bassanio? 'Happiest of all is that her gentle spirit commits itself to yours to be directed, as from her lord, her governor, her king.' Doesn't that prove something?"

Elizabeth bit her lip in vexation.

"And of course Milton makes a similar statement," the student continued, "when his ideal woman says to Adam, 'God thy law; thou mine!'"

"As members of the male sex, Milton and Shakespeare naturally claimed their superiority," Elizabeth contended, wishing she could cite some woman writer who stated in ringing sentences the superiority—or at least the equality—of woman.

"Look about you," the student continued. "Do you see women holding positions of importance in government, medicine, or law?"

"If there are none, it is because men have reserved those fields for themselves," Elizabeth stated, trying to hide her rancor.

"Can you cite any law that excludes women from the professions?" he asked.

Elizabeth hesitated. Unless she could give the name and date of a legislative act or legal precedent, she might as well be silent. "I move we declare a recess," she said, "and resume our discussion later."

The young man laughed and strode off toward the court-house with a satisfied air. Elizabeth hurried to her father's office and was pleased to find him alone.

Daniel Cady was sitting at his desk, a closely written document before him. He looked up at her approach, a smile on his usually stern face.

"Ah, Elizabeth, what brings you here? It's been some time since you've come to see me. You appear to be entirely occupied with parties and picnicking of late."

It was on the tip of Elizabeth's tongue to ask what else there was for her to do, barred as she was from every serious pursuit. She took care of her room and clothing, helped her mother entertain numerous guests, read all she could lay her hands on, wrote extensive letters, and often went visiting at the homes of friends and relatives. Sometimes it seemed that the only worthwhile thing she did was teach a Sunday School class of young Negroes. From time to time, goaded beyond endurance by the students in her father's law office, she spent hours reading law.

The more she studied, the more aware she became of woman's inferior position. When the family's laundress came to Mr. Cady in tears because her husband had given their son for adoption to a couple going West, and she would probably never see him again, Elizabeth was nearly sick with fury. She knew what her father would say. The law states that the husband has full control over the children.

Again, when a neighbor woman, mother of three beautiful little girls, came secretly to the office, Elizabeth suspected that she would receive no legal aid. Her husband, the neighbor said, was so furious that the children were female that he beat and abused her mercilessly.

"Unless he struck you with a weapon more than an inch in diameter, there is no redress for you under the present laws," Mr. Cady said. "A man has a legal right to chastise his wife."

The situation in regard to woman was so depressing that Elizabeth had not opened a lawbook in weeks. Moreover, studying without a goal was in itself discouraging. What good would it do her to learn all the law in the world? She would not be permitted to use her knowledge. The barriers restricting women infuriated her more than ever.

But there was no point in antagonizing Father with a recital of her frustrations. His smile aroused all her childhood love for him. She longed again to compensate in some way for the loss of Eleazer.

"I need some legal help, Father, something to show why women are excluded from the professions. Can you help me?"

Daniel Cady sighed and leaned back. "I've already gone over with you the position of women in English law, which holds for women in this country, too. Blackstone in his *Commentaries* states that women live under the shadow of a 'defect of sex.'"

"And that defect of sex is reflected in the laws relating to women's property, their children, their work, their marriage, even the conventions and traditions that have grown up about their mental ability and their place in society," Elizabeth said.

"You could put it that way," Father commented. "Custom is strong. It has decreed that woman by nature of her sex is not able to meet the intellectual demands of the world's work, and so must be spared the stresses and responsibilities that men are more suited to undertake."

Elizabeth sighed. "I think women could do a lot more than they do now if they only had the chance. Those old laws were formed by a society in which a woman's chief duty was to produce children so that estates could be handed down from one generation to another."

"Some people still hold that opinion," Father said gently.

Elizabeth flushed. She was twenty-three now, seven years older than Mother had been when she was married. Hattie was Mrs. Daniel Eaton, living in New York City, and the mother of a son and daughter. Her cousin Libby was promised to Charles Dudley Miller. Most of Elizabeth's friends had husbands and children. And she was tired of remarks about her spinster state.

"I'm not even sure that I want to be married," she said.

Her father raised his eyebrows. "My dear!" he exclaimed. "Of course you will marry. It's a natural and proper step."

"A downward step, it seems to me," Elizabeth said. "How can you advocate it when right here in your office I have seen the disadvantages of marriage?"

"You have seen *what?*" Daniel Cady demanded.

"All those wives and widows who come in here to see

you, asking that their property be restored to them, that
their children be given into their custody, that they be freed
from a tie that is demeaning and dangerous—wouldn't
you say they were witnesses to the inferior state of woman
in marriage?"

"Oh, Elizabeth, those women had made poor choices.
Their husbands were dissolute or misguided or given over to
drink. I am sure you would have better judgment in your
choice of a partner."

"A partner?" Elizabeth demanded. "What kind of a partnership is it when one member has every power? When a
woman marries she loses all right to hold property; everything she owns becomes the property of her husband. If she
has children, and her husband wishes to give them away for
adoption, she has no power to prevent him. If he consumes
liquor to the point of drunkenness and forces her to satisfy
his physical demands, she has no legal right to resist."

Daniel Cady's brows drew down over his eyes. "Elizabeth!" he thundered. "What a shocking thing for a young
lady to say!"

Elizabeth could feel her face flaming. "It's true, isn't it?"

"Yes, but the subject is not discussed in polite society."
His voice rang out with authority. Elizabeth knew she had
gone far enough. Too far, in fact. For a moment she sat quietly. Then she said softly, "I really do worry about the legal
side of marriage, Father."

"If you choose wisely, you need have no fears. Your
sisters' husbands are apparently giving them no difficulty."

Father was right. Dan Eaton was a fine person, beloved by
all the family. As for Edward Bayard, there was no more
noble or generous-hearted person alive, Elizabeth was sure.

How grateful she was to him for choosing new and worth-while books for her to read and study, for leading philosoph-ical discussions, for directing her thoughts into broadening channels.

If only— She pushed the thought away. Edward was married to Tryphena. It was wrong for her to think of him as anything but a brother-in-law. Perhaps someday she would meet someone as wonderful as he.

Leaving the office, she met Madge in her riding habit, tall and beautiful, her chestnut hair caught back in a net.

"Oh, Liz, I've been looking everywhere for you," Madge cried. "Won't you come for a ride?"

"I'll be ready in a minute," Elizabeth promised, and ran up the stairs.

As the two sisters rode over the Johnstown hills, breath-ing in the fragrant spring air, delighting in the fresh green of trees and shrubs, Elizabeth told of her encounter with the newly arrived law student.

"Oh, these men—aren't they infuriating?" Madge said. "You just leave him to me. I'll have Peter saddle Old Bony for him tomorrow, and give him a good shaking up."

"And I might challenge him to a game of chess!" Eliza-beth said, laughing.

That evening Elizabeth demurely invited the young law-yer to a game. He accepted with alacrity, eager to display his prowess. Elizabeth planned her moves carefully, using a series of steps Edward had taught her. Then she made one final play, and said quietly, "Checkmate." Her adversary stared at her, dumfounded.

The next day Madge asked him if he would like to go rid-ing with her. He was so jounced and joggled by Old Bony's

labored gait as he strove to keep up with Madge's swift mare
that Peter had to help him from his mount, and he spent the
next day in his room, nursing his aching bones.

From that time on he made no more mention of masculine
superiority.

The victory, if such it was, far from satisfied Elizabeth.
She spent hours reading the books in her father's office,
trying to find out more about the laws that discriminated
against women.

Sometimes she would read her slim, leather-bound copy
of *Alcuin* by Charles Brockden Brown that Gerrit Smith
had given her on one of his visits. It was a bitter satisfaction
to discover in its pages, written in 1798, a recital of the same
injustices that were still plaguing women.

"Women are defective," she read. "They are seldom or
never metaphysicians, chemists, or lawgivers." The last
word stung her to the quick. What would she not give to be
a lawyer! She read on: "Why? Because they are sempstresses
and cooks. . . . They cannot read who never saw an alphabet. They who know no tool but the needle cannot be skillful at the pen." Of course that was true. Weren't all girls
taught that it was more important to sew well than to write
clearly?

The next words seemed to jump out of the page and burn
themselves into her mind: "Of all forms of injustice, that is
the most egregious which makes . . . sex a reason for ex-
cluding one half of mankind from all those paths which lead
to usefulness and honor."

Here was the very same thought that constantly exasperated her. Was there no path that for her would lead to usefulness and honor?

Elizabeth suspected that her mother shared some of her views. But it was difficult to talk with Mother, whose sense of propriety and loyalty to Father kept her from discussing any subject upon which they might disagree.

Then an incident occurred which made Elizabeth feel closer to her mother than ever before. In the choice of a new pastor for the Johnstown Presbyterian Church the membership was divided, the women favoring one candidate and the men another. Elizabeth liked neither, thinking that both men lacked the wisdom and kindliness of dear old Dr. Hosack who had died several years before. It was rumored that at the time of voting the women's ballots would be separated from the men's and then disregarded. A delegation of church women called upon Margaret Cady.

On the appointed day the members convened in the church. Elizabeth and Madge accompanied their parents. As was customary the men voted first, walking up the central aisle, one by one, to place their folded slips in a large urn in front of the altar. Then it was time for the women. They trod the same path, each in turn depositing her ballot.

Elizabeth noted that Mother had arranged to be the last of the women to vote. Slowly she walked toward the altar, and when she reached the urn, she placed her ballot on top of all the others. Then to the amazement of Elizabeth and almost everyone else, she stooped down from her height of six feet, and with her long, strong arm, stirred the contents around and around, until the votes of men and women were mingled beyond the chance of any separation. Then in majestic dignity she returned to her place.

A counting of the votes revealed that the minister favored by the women had been chosen. Elizabeth felt like shouting in triumph—not for his election, but for her mother's action.

At home little was said about the incident. Mother's only comment was, "There are more ways than one of skinning a cat. And it was important to have a *fair* election."

Frequent letters came from Peterboro, urging Elizabeth to visit. Libby sent a copy of *The Liberator*, William Lloyd Garrison's newspaper, containing one of his impassioned pleas for the abolition of slavery. Elizabeth showed it to her mother. Her eyes lit up, and she said, "It will come—in time."

When Daniel Cady picked up the paper, his face darkened. "That man Garrison is an incendiary. No wonder the responsible businessmen of Boston mobbed him. He and his fellow abolitionists are a threat to our country, attacking it in such a manner. If they do not agree with the laws about slavery, they should try to change them, not disobey them."

"If you could have seen that slave girl at Peterboro, you might feel differently," Elizabeth said.

"I would have felt it my duty to enforce the law," Daniel Cady said sternly.

Elizabeth was about to retort when she saw her mother put a finger to her lips and shake her head in warning. It's no use, Elizabeth thought. Father has his ideas, and I have mine, and we are both convinced that we are in the right.

At summer's end the young law student proposed to Elizabeth. As gently as possible, for she had come to know him as an able and cheerful adversary, she declined his offer.

Later her father, whom the young man had approached for permission to seek her hand, questioned her as to her refusal.

"He comes of a good family, has a keen mind, and will go far. Why did you turn him down?" he asked.

"Because of his views about women, for one thing," Elizabeth answered.

"It seemed to me that he had altered his attitude considerably of late," Father said drily, his eyes twinkling.

"Yes, I had noticed, too," Elizabeth agreed, smiling. "The real reason I don't wish to marry him is simply that I don't love him."

"Perhaps you would learn to love him in time. He is a very eligible young man."

"That's not enough for me," Elizabeth said, hurrying from the room so that Father would not see her tears. Would she never meet a man who measured up to all her expectations?

Long ago she had made up her mind that unless marriage could be an equal partnership, she would not enter into it. And where would she find anyone who would look favorably upon such an agreement? She wished she could talk over her problem with someone. But in all Johnstown there was no one in whom she cared to confide. Tryphena and Edward had moved to Seneca Falls, and she rarely saw Edward for the long, serious talks they had once shared.

It was awkward to face her rejected suitor daily. His doleful mien was embarrassing. And her father's reproachful gaze depressed and irritated her. Johnstown began to get on her nerves.

Suddenly Elizabeth decided that she must get away. Perhaps in a different setting she would gain a new perspective and find a solution to the gnawing problem of what she might do with her life.

What better people to discuss the question with than her beloved Smith cousins? Early in September of 1839 she set out for Peterboro.

7
NEW WINDOWS OPENING

*E*lizabeth arrived at Peterboro to find the household pulsating with activity. So many guests arrived and departed daily that the Smiths' home seemed almost like an inn. Many visitors were youthful friends of Libby's. Others were people involved in the reform causes which Gerrit Smith supported.

Elizabeth happily took part in the regime of healthful exercise for body and mind, with daily walks and rides in the countryside alternating with periods of reading and discussion. What fun it was in the evening to sing in a group, or whirl over the polished floors with one partner after another. Determinedly she threw herself into every activity, thankful to have left behind the tensions of Johnstown.

A few days after her arrival, Elizabeth had a quiet hour with Gerrit and Nancy and an opportunity to voice her mounting discontent with the many restrictions imposed upon her and all women.

"What's the use of being born with some degree of intelligence," she demanded, "if we're to be denied the opportunity to make some worthwhile use of it?"

Gerrit held up the newspaper he had been reading. "Surely you have seen accounts of what women are doing in the antislavery cause," he remarked. "Look at Lucretia Mott, Lydia Maria Child, and the Grimké sisters. They are using their intelligence to win thousands over to abolition."

Anyone who could read must know about those women, thought Elizabeth. Lucretia Mott was the Philadelphia Quaker who had become noted for her eloquent attacks upon slavery. Lydia Maria Child was the widely read Massachusetts author who had sacrificed her popularity with the publication of her book *An Appeal in Favor of That Class of Americans Called Africans*. Sarah and Angelina Grimké, former wealthy aristocrats from South Carolina who had freed their slaves and become Quakers, had mounted the lecture platform in their zeal for abolition, and drew large crowds wherever they spoke. Angelina had last year become the wife of Theodore Weld, one of the growing number of antislavery workers which included men such as William Lloyd Garrison, James G. Birney, John Greenleaf Whittier, and Charles Sumner.

Strife over slavery had been prominent in the news for years, especially since Great Britain's emancipation of its slaves in 1833, and the first National Anti-Slavery Convention in Philadelphia a few months later. Most newspapers had carried the full text of the convention's bold denunciation of slavery, the *Declaration of Sentiments*. Since then the country had been flooded by articles and broadsides, among them John Greenleaf Whittier's poem "Our Countrymen in Chains." A framed copy hung on the wall opposite Elizabeth, the face of its pictured slave reminding her of Peter, her friend from childhood.

When she read about the unbridled violence which threatened abolitionists everywhere, Elizabeth could not help but be alarmed. In Boston William Lloyd Garrison had been dragged through the streets with a rope around his neck.

At Alton, Illinois, an antislavery publisher, Elijah P. Love-
joy, had been mobbed and killed. And hardly had the
national antislavery headquarters, Pennsylvania Hall in Philadelphia, been dedicated when a mob stormed it and burned
it to the ground.

She might as well forget her own problem, Elizabeth
thought. Cousin Gerrit was so wrapped up in abolition
that for the present he was deaf and blind to the need for
reform in other areas, such as the status of women.

"Is there any way that I could aid the antislavery cause?"
Elizabeth asked.

Gerrit hesitated. He's wondering what Father would say,
Elizabeth thought.

"You could inform yourself as to its progress," Gerrit
suggested. "That would be a first step."

Eagerly Elizabeth threw herself into the task. The library at Peterboro was a storehouse of material, for Cousin
Gerrit subscribed to numerous antislavery periodicals. Elizabeth became familiar with the work of the American Anti-
Slavery Society and the names of the men in its publications
office in New York. Some of them she recognized—Birney,
Weld, and Whittier. A new name to her was that of Henry B.
Stanton, who was, she learned, not only a gifted writer, but
an eloquent speaker against slavery.

One morning Libby came to Elizabeth in great excitement. "Did you know that Henry B. Stanton is coming here
to stay while he gives a series of lectures on temperance
and abolition? Isn't that exciting?"

"Indeed it is!" Elizabeth agreed. It would be a privilege
to meet face to face one of the courageous men who risked

their lives every time they mounted the platform. She en-
visioned a baldish man with long white whiskers and a quav-
ering voice.

That afternoon a group of guests arrived from Utica.
Mr. Stanton could not be among them, for they were all
fairly young, Elizabeth and Libby decided, peering out
from an upstairs window. As they watched, a tall, thin man
in his thirties, with a long face and aquiline nose, leaped
out of the carriage and gallantly helped a young lady to
alight.

"That's Miss Stewart," Libby whispered. "She's engaged to
be married."

"Is that so?" Elizabeth remarked. She was not interested
in Miss Stewart, beauty though she was. It was the man who
was handing her down who caught Elizabeth's eyes. She
had never before seen such ebullient vitality or a face that
shone with more good humor. She was about to ask his name,
then decided not to. He was Miss Stewart's fiancé. It would
seem strange if Elizabeth should show interest in him.

Gerrit's voice floated up to them. "My dear Stanton, it is
indeed an honor to have so distinguished a speaker as yourself here under our roof."

Had she heard correctly? Elizabeth wondered. This was
surely not the venerable lecturer she had pictured. A second
later she heard Nancy say, "Welcome to Peterboro, Mr.
Stanton." It could be no other.

At the dinner table that evening, Elizabeth found herself
seated across from Mr. Stanton. Under her eager questioning
he talked of his famous associates, enlivening his account
with anecdotes. He told her that one time when he and

Whittier were scheduled to speak in Newburyport, no hall or church was available, so fearful were people of the damage that might be done by mobs. The meeting was held outdoors in a garden. A hostile crowd surrounded the speakers, who managed eventually to get away safely, but not before someone had torn all the buttons off Stanton's coat.

"Tell about the time you nearly lost your life, when three-inch-thick boards had to be spiked over the windows," one of the young men urged.

"There must be more interesting topics of conversation," Mr. Stanton said. "Has anyone read Mrs. Child's latest book, *Authentic Narratives of American Slavery?*"

Elizabeth listened to Henry Stanton, entranced. Here was a man who not only knew and associated with the famous abolitionists about whom she had read, but was himself a noted worker for that cause. She felt that Henry Stanton was opening a door for her into a new world of daring and sacrifice, peopled by champions of the oppressed. To her this dedicated orator seemed a modern-day knight on a sacred mission, going forth to battle the dragons of evil with no weapon save his persuasive pen and tongue. When dinner ended, Elizabeth hardly knew what food had been served or whether she had consumed any.

The next morning Elizabeth was among the party of young women and men who rode in two carriages from Peterboro to a neighboring town for an all-day convention. She sat in the front row between Libby and Miss Stewart. She could hardly wait for Henry Stanton to speak.

On the platform he proved himself a superb orator, his eyes beneath their shaggy brows seeming to shoot forth sparks.

He provoked laughter, appealed to reason, and finally drew tears from his audience as he painted a verbal picture of the harrowing conditions of slavery.

Elizabeth thought she had never heard a speaker so eloquent and moving. If there was a slight unevenness in his delivery, Mr. Stanton made up for it by a sincerity of feeling that went to his listeners' hearts.

Had she been the most dyed-in-the-wool advocate of slavery before she heard his speech, Elizabeth was certain that she would have been won over to the cause of abolition. Already convinced of the rightness of the antislavery movement, her belief was strengthened by his arguments. What she would not give to be able to move audiences in such a fashion!

That evening Elizabeth had another dinner partner, but when the meal was over she sought Mr. Stanton. Enthusiastically she complimented him upon his speech.

"You did not think the scene I described was so sordid as to be offensive to the audience?" he asked.

"How could it be?" she retorted. "It was not nearly so frightful as some other experiences." Almost before she knew it she was telling him about the slave, Harriet. When she had finished, she put one hand to her cheek. She could almost hear her mother exclaiming in mortification that a slave's experiences with her master should not be discussed with a gentleman.

If Mr. Stanton was shocked, he did not show it. "Every advocate of slavery should meet a slave so mistreated," he said. "Then the cause of abolition would be easily won."

At that moment Miss Stewart came up and invited him to

join a group at the piano. Elizabeth watched them walk across the room together, feeling an unaccustomed pang of envy. Life would never be dull with a partner like Henry Stanton.

A week passed by. Each day the young men and women of the Peterboro household went off to hear antislavery or temperance lectures, often returning late at night in the bright moonlight.

When it was Henry Stanton's turn to speak, Elizabeth could not help a quickening of her pulse. It was thrilling to feel the enthusiasm of the crowds at the meetings in response to his oratory. There was such force, such persuasion in his words. How could anyone hear him and not be won over to the cause of temperance or abolition?

One day Mr. Stanton was delivering a temperance lecture on a platform covered by a piece of linoleum that protruded some three inches over the edge of the boards in front. In the midst of one of his most eloquent passages, he compared the inebriate's downward course to the Falls of Niagara and the struggle with drink to the hopeless efforts of a man in the rapids.

Just as he described the fatal plunge over the precipice, he advanced to the edge of the platform. The linoleum gave way under his feet, and in an instant he went headlong into the audience, carrying with him desk, glass, pitcher, and water.

Elizabeth gasped in dismay. Had Mr. Stanton been hurt? To her relief he was back on the platform again almost immediately, remarking with great coolness, "I carried my illustration further than I had intended. Yet even so the drunkard falls, glass in hand, carrying destruction with him. But not so readily does he rise again from the terrible depths into which he has precipitated himself."

The whole house cheered again and again. Elizabeth, clapping until her hands stung, thought she had never seen a braver recovery from what some men might have found a disaster.

At the week's end, Miss Stewart returned to Utica.

"Why should she go now," Elizabeth asked Nancy, "right in the middle of the lecture series?"

Nancy smiled. "She is going home to prepare for her wedding to Luther Marsh. Hadn't you heard that she was engaged to him?"

Elizabeth could feel the red rising to her cheeks. "I had heard she was engaged," she stammered, "but I thought it was to—to someone else."

In the weeks that followed, Henry Stanton often chose to ride in the same carriage with Elizabeth, and directed many of his remarks in her direction. She enjoyed the swift give-and-take of verbal skirmishes with him, the stimulation of fencing with ideas. Often she did not need to finish a sentence before he caught her meaning, or she would sense what he was about to say.

One evening Elizabeth was putting Gerrit's handsomely carved chessmen in place on the board, when Henry Stanton asked if he might play with her. For a moment she was tempted to lay aside her hard-won skill. Men did not like to be beaten, she knew. But her nature was to be honest and direct. She would not stoop to subterfuge now.

Before many moves, Elizabeth realized that in Henry Stanton she had an able opponent. The game became a duel of wits. At length, by employing a gambit she had learned from Edward, she outmaneuvered her opponent, forcing him into a position from which he had no alternative but to capitulate.

As he surveyed the board, Henry Stanton drew his brows together in exasperation. Then he picked up his king in his long, thin fingers, and inclining his head in a slight bow, held out the piece to her. "You have forced me to surrender, Miss Cady, but the bitterness of defeat is alleviated by the pleasure of having an antagonist so young, so charming, and so intelligent!" He gave her an amiable grin. "It is not often I have a chance to play with anyone so skillful. May I challenge you to another game tomorrow evening?"

How different from the usual masculine discomfiture at losing to a woman! Elizabeth could not help but admire his attitude. The following evening when he bested her after a tense struggle, she was almost glad to acknowledge defeat. He deserved to win!

The fact that Henry Stanton was ten years older than Elizabeth did not make him less attractive in her eyes. He was the same age as Edward Bayard, and he was the first man she had met who seemed to possess all of Edward's fine qualities—perhaps even more.

As they grew to know each other better, Elizabeth marveled that two people could share so many views on controversial subjects. Henry believed that women should be able to pursue higher education, and that Oberlin College had the right idea when it opened its doors to female students in 1833. He felt that many laws were unfair to women. He even went so far as to state that women should be allowed more participation in business affairs.

Henry confided in Elizabeth his deep commitment to reform work and the great value he placed upon the friendships he had made in the abolition movement. From his pocket he drew a slender volume and held it out to her, opened at an inscription.

The book was a collection of John Greenleaf Whittier's poems, published in 1838. In it the poet had written, "Dedicated to Henry B. Stanton as a token of the author's personal friendship, and of his respect for the unreserved devotion of exalted talents to the cause of humanity and freedom."

"Those words mean more to me than pages of flowery praise," Henry said with quiet pride.

One morning Elizabeth was walking up and down on the piazza after breakfast. The air had never seemed so fragrant nor the foliage so colorful. What a glorious Indian summer this was.

Hearing footsteps behind her, she turned to see Henry Stanton's tall figure.

"This is my first free day in weeks without a speaking engagement," he said. "I can't think of a more enjoyable way to spend it than by going for a horseback ride over the hills with you. Would you be willing to accompany me?"

Elizabeth hurriedly stammered her assent, and went to change. Why was she so nervous? She had had scores of similar invitations from other men. Even her fingers felt unnatural as she fumbled with the fastenings of her long riding skirt.

On the ride through the idyllic autumn scenery, Elizabeth's nervousness increased. Henry, usually so eloquent, was this morning nearly silent. For mile after mile he made only brief replies to her desperate attempts at conversation. Each time she stole a glance at him, he seemed absorbed in his thoughts. Was he bored with her company?

On the homeward ride, as they reached a grove of golden-leaved maples, Henry reached over and caught the bridle of Elizabeth's horse.

Reining in her mare, she glanced at him in puzzlement. To her surprise she saw that his eyes were imploring in their intensity.

"Elizabeth, my dearest, haven't you guessed how I feel about you?" he said in great agitation. "Say that there's some chance for me."

What was this soaring happiness that was sweeping her up and up into the clouds? "Oh, Henry," she whispered.

Then he was on the ground, helping her from her mount, and they were clinging together, his lips on hers, tentatively at first, then possessively.

Before they returned to Peterboro she had consented to become his wife.

8

TAKE OUT THE WORD *OBEY*

$\mathscr{O}$f course you realize that your father will never consent to your marriage to Henry Stanton," Gerrit said solemnly to Elizabeth in his study the following morning. Henry had gone off to a meeting. Elizabeth could still feel the pressure of his fingers on hers as he had said good-by in the presence of family and guests, only the ardor of his gaze betraying his emotion.

"Why shouldn't Father consent?" Elizabeth demanded. "Henry has all the qualities I've ever hoped for in a husband."

"But he is an *abolitionist*," Gerrit said. "Need I remind you of your father's deep aversion to anyone connected with the antislavery movement?"

"Except you," Elizabeth interposed, thinking that Cousin Gerrit's wealth and position made acceptable his involvement in any cause, however radical. "Don't you think that Father will change his mind after he meets Henry?"

"Have you ever known your father to set aside principle for an individual?" Gerrit countered.

Cudgel her brain as she might, Elizabeth could not recall one such incident.

"Please reconsider this engagement, Elizabeth. Your acquaintance with Mr. Stanton has been very brief. Don't take a hasty step into what may be an unsatisfactory marriage."

"How can it be so?" Elizabeth cried. "I've never known a

more agreeable companion." Nor been so in love, she added to herself. The mere thought of Henry sent the blood racing through her veins.

"Financially he is in no position to provide you with the kind of life you now enjoy. His earnings are modest, and he has no prospect of inheriting substantial means."

"Who cares about money?" Elizabeth asked, tossing her head.

"Your father, for one. He would not like to see you in want."

"Henry is perfectly capable of supporting me," Elizabeth stormed. "Cousin Gerrit, I think you are being very unkind."

Gerrit threw her a troubled glance. "I feel a special responsibility because you have fallen in love while a guest at my home. Your parents expect you to make a suitable alliance with a man solidly established in business or a profession. I am sure they will be disturbed."

How could anyone who knew Henry speak in this way? Especially Cousin Gerrit, whom she was counting upon for support? Elizabeth was about to burst out in protest, when Gerrit held up his hand.

"It might be wise for you to write your parents now about your plans. By the time you return home they will have had time to get over their initial surprise and certain displeasure."

Greatly agitated, Elizabeth left the study, and wrote to her parents. She told them of Henry's direct descent from Elder Brewster of the *Mayflower*; his schooling in the Academy at Jewett City, Connecticut; his later study of law and the classics; and his enrollment in the Lane Theological

Seminary in Cincinnati, which he had left in order to work against slavery. Henry was a mature man of thirty-four and possessed of the same qualities that Father had lauded in the young lawyer whose proposal she had recently rejected. Like him, Henry Stanton came of a good family, had a keen mind, and would go far.

One day followed another, and no reply came from Johnstown. Each afternoon Elizabeth eagerly searched through the neat pile of mail on the hall table, then turned away in disappointment.

Indian summer was waning when Elizabeth drove homeward. The day before she had reluctantly parted from Henry Stanton, who was bound for a distant part of the state on a continuance of his lecture tour.

On the evening of her arrival in Johnstown, her father invited her into his office.

"What madness impelled you to cast in your lot with a journalist and rabble-rouser?" Daniel Cady demanded. "Don't you realize that you are related to some of the most distinguished people in the country? Your mother's family own a large part of New York State. As for myself, I've gained a certain eminence, although it goes against my nature to mention it. But I must remind you that as my daughter you will inherit no small fortune. And I do not wish to see my hard-earned substance scattered to the winds in a futile, foolish attempt to take legally acquired property away from southern slaveholders. No, I most certainly will not countenance your marriage to a radical such as Henry Stanton."

Elizabeth had sat in angry silence during her father's speech. Now she burst forth, "How can you say that when you don't even know him? The important thing is that I *love* Henry!"

"There's a great deal more to marriage than love," Daniel Cady said darkly.

"Not for me!" Elizabeth declared. "Henry is the only man I shall ever marry."

Autumn, gray and forbidding, deepened into winter. Its cold was no less icy than the chill between Elizabeth and her father. No matter how passionately she pleaded Henry's cause, Daniel Cady remained obdurate. The match was utterly unsuitable. He would not approve.

"You don't like Henry because he is an abolitionist," Elizabeth stormed. "But Cousin Gerrit is one, and I'm sure that Mother shares his opinions."

Daniel Cady gave her a searing glance. She had better not mention again her mother's antislavery leanings.

"It is not Mr. Stanton's beliefs I question," Father said stiffly, "but whether or not he will be able to support you."

That night Elizabeth wrote a long letter to Henry, pouring out her disappointment at her father's attitude. If there were only some way he could be convinced of Henry's ability.

By return mail came a letter.

New York, January 4, 1840

DEAR ELIZABETH—

Since I was thirteen years old I have been thrown entirely upon my own resources, especially as to money. I have never received a dollar's gratuitous aid from anyone, though it has been frequently pressed upon me. I always declined it, because I knew it would relax my perseverance and detract from my self-reliance, and because I was aware that if I would be a man, I must build on my own foundation with my own hands. Since

I was thirteen, I have spent about eight years in study, and during this time defrayed all my expenses; have assisted two brothers in acquiring a liberal education; have expended something for a library, etc., and too much perhaps for mere gratification; have been rather liberal in my contributions, giving freely to the missionary, Bible, temperance, and antislavery causes; have sustained some pecuniary losses; been the victim of ill health one entire year; and though I never made the getting of money for its own sake an object, I have saved from these expenditures about $3,000 in cash. During this time I have met and surmounted obstacles before which many would have quailed. You may ask by what means I obtained the necessary funds to do this. I answer by the hands, the tongue, the pen, and the ingenuity of a New Englander, trained up by a mother who is the great-great-great-granddaughter of a man who set his foot on Plymouth Rock in 1620.

LOVINGLY,
Henry

Elizabeth scanned the sheet eagerly, then tossed it angrily on her dressing table. What kind of a love letter was this? No tender phrase, no avowal of affection, not even a word of encouragement to her to stand firm against her father's opposition.

Suddenly she perceived Henry's purpose. The letter itself was her encouragement. It was intended for her father's eye.

But when she showed it to Daniel Cady, his only comment was, "Three thousand dollars—pshaw!" He remained inflexible.

Only Henry's subsequent missives, intended for Elizabeth's eyes alone, each one declaring his love, each one painting a bright and joyous future for them, kept Elizabeth from giving in completely to despair.

As weeks lengthened into months, Elizabeth's resolve

weakened. Tryphena and Edward came for a visit, and aligned themselves stoutly with Daniel Cady. Elizabeth had been taken in by Mr. Stanton's eloquence, Tryphena said. One could not live on fine phrases. A good bank balance was a better foundation.

Elizabeth had never felt so torn. Her family was here. Henry was far away. Sometimes she could hardly recall his face. At length family pressures were effective. In a miasma of fear and uncertainty she wrote to Henry, breaking their engagement.

To her amazement, Henry did not respond as a rejected suitor. Instead he renewed his protestations of deep love, re-affirmed his ability to support her, and begged that she re-consider her decision. For weeks she resisted his pleas.

Then came another letter from Henry. He had been chosen to go to England as a delegate to the World's Anti-Slavery Convention. It was an honor to be included with such men as Wendell Phillips, William Lloyd Garri-son, and James Birney, and he should rightly be elated at the prospect. But, he wrote, he could not bear the prospect of being further separated from Elizabeth by the broad Atlantic Ocean. Would she not reconsider, and accompany him on the journey?

Many American women were being sent to London, also, as delegates from various female antislavery societies, he added, naming Lucretia Mott, Ann Phillips, Abby South-wick, and Mary Grew. Elizabeth would not lack for stimu-lating feminine companionship.

Elizabeth recalled the last time she had visited Harriet and Daniel Eaton in New York, and had looked out across the ocean. It was too vast an expanse to come between her and the man she loved. No, she could not remain in Johnstown. Filial ties were not enough.

Suddenly Elizabeth's course seemed crystal clear. No matter how firmly her father and family opposed the match, she could not view the future as anything but bleak and lonely without Henry. The door into the world of reform that he had unlocked for her last autumn was now opening wide. Here was an opportunity to step over its threshold and mingle with the valiant souls working there. Most important of all, she would go as Henry's wife.

When Elizabeth informed her parents that she was going to be married within the month, they took the news with surprising calm. They must have guessed, she suspected, that if they had not given their consent she would have gone off without it.

With no time for the customary lengthy wedding preparations, Elizabeth packed her clothes, put aside a white evening gown for her wedding dress, and went to see the Reverend Hugh Maire at the Presbyterian Church. There was an important matter she must settle with him, one that she and Henry had discussed and agreed upon early in their engagement.

The Scottish clergyman was aghast. "Ye want me to perform a marriage ceremony and *leave out the word 'obey'?*" he sputtered. "But, lass, such a thing has ne'er been done before! Dinna ye wish to obey the man ye love?"

"Indeed I do not," Elizabeth stated firmly. "Our marriage is to be a partnership—of equals. You would not want my husband to have to swear to obey *me*, would you?"

For a moment she was afraid that the stout little man

would have an apoplectic fit or would refuse to marry them at all. But at length he agreed to accede to her wishes.

The wedding was scheduled for Thursday, the tenth of May. On the way from New York City, Henry's boat ran aground, and he did not reach Johnstown until May 11. The Reverend Mr. Maire demanded that the ceremony be put off until Saturday, as Friday was considered unlucky for a marriage.

Was superstition to dictate the date of her wedding? Elizabeth, already tense at the first strained meeting between Henry and her parents, was ready to explode with fury.

Together Elizabeth and Henry talked to the clergyman, insisting that they be married on Friday since they were to sail from New York for England early the next week, and they needed all available time to reach their ship by its scheduled departure date.

Again the Scotsman capitulated.

The ceremony took place without untoward incident in the Cady home in the presence of the family and a few close friends.

9

WOMEN DELEGATES BARRED

*F*rom her seat in Freemasons' Hall in London, Elizabeth angrily awaited the formal opening of the World's Anti-Slavery Convention on June 12, 1840. The vast auditorium was nearly a hundred feet long, its walls were hung with portraits of illustrious Masons, and its two thousand seats were occupied by delegates from many parts of the world.

All that Elizabeth could see, however, was the lofty ceiling and the strained faces of women around her, like herself confined within a curtained area from which they could view little of the proceedings. Shut within this space, they must wait while the male delegates decided whether or not women would be allowed to participate in the meetings. The men disregarded completely the fact that the women delegates had been duly elected by American antislavery societies as their representatives.

Just ahead of Elizabeth was a place where the curtains came together. How she longed to reach forward and pull them apart for a look at the assemblage. But Lucretia Mott was sitting beside her, and Elizabeth knew that Lucretia would consider such conduct undignified.

Nantucket born, Lucretia was one of the Quaker Coffins whose men had captained ships to distant ports on voyages of a year or more, while their wives, shouldering the responsibility of home and family, grew independent in thought and action. That heritage Lucretia had developed, stating her arguments against slavery at public meetings with such clarity and courage that she was now an acknowledged leader in the American antislavery movement—and one of the delegates whose admission was in question because of her sex.

Of all the women delegates whom Elizabeth had met in the week preceding the convention, she admired the Quaker most of all. Not for Lucretia's beauty, although her classic features were flawless. Nor for her warmth of spirit, which reached out to everyone with whom she came in contact. Nor even for her clear, precise method of speaking, which won over listeners by the score.

Lucretia's intelligence was what Elizabeth found fascinating, her ability to see through to the heart of a problem and present a solution at once simple and ingenious. It was an education in itself to hear her propound a theory, and cite a series of logical arguments in its defense, whether the subject be politics, religion, or reform.

If Elizabeth must sit here in this cloistered indignity, at least she was with Lucretia, who was fifteen years older and had faced many humiliating situations in her career as preacher and reformer. If only she possessed some of the Quaker woman's serenity!

Inwardly Elizabeth was seething with rage. It was bad enough that the English delegates wished to bar women from participation in the convention, simply because in England women could not take equal part with men in reform associations. It was even worse that half the American delegates, the political abolitionists, took the same position.

The leader of that group, James G. Birney, had made the eighteen-day Atlantic crossing with Henry and Elizabeth on

the sailing ship *Montreal,* and during the voyage Elizabeth
had grown to dislike him intensely. She had tried to be
pleasant, because he was engaged to Cousin Nancy's sister
and because he was the presidential candidate of the Liberty
party, of which Cousin Gerrit was the principal financial
backer. While at sea Mr. Birney had continually sought out
Elizabeth and Henry, even when they least desired his company. He seemed to forget that the trip was also their hon-
eymoon.

Elizabeth's initial antipathy had deepened daily as Mr.
Birney found fault with her actions. He criticized her for
calling Henry by his first name instead of Mr. Stanton, as
was socially correct and, in her opinion, unbearably stuffy.
He openly chided her for being hauled up to the masthead
in a boatswain's chair, an experience he deemed extremely
unladylike. She had been terrified at the height, especially
when the ship rolled and she in her perch swung out over
the blue depths, with nothing beneath but white caps and in-
digo water. But safely on deck again, with Henry's arm
strong and solid beneath her trembling hand, she would not
admit her fear to the men and made light of the experience.

What troubled Elizabeth chiefly at the moment was that
Henry was a member of the same political abolitionist group
as Mr. Birney. How far he would go in his support of their
theories she dared not guess.

If Henry should stand up and speak in objection to
women as delegates—what would she do? It could be the
end of their marriage. She could never live in harmony with
a man who denied equal participation to women. Yet the
thought of life without Henry filled her with desolation.

Thank heaven some of the Americans favored whole-

heartedly the right of women to take part. They were called
Garrisonians, after William Lloyd Garrison. Elizabeth's
heart was with that group, as it would be with any faction
that favored the emancipation of women from fetters of the
past, be they political, religious, or social.

Now the chairman's gavel sounded. Impatiently Elizabeth
waited through the introductions. How long-winded these
men could be, and as pompous as if they were the lords of
creation!

Thomas Clarkson, the veteran English abolitionist, made
the opening address. Then another speaker began. There
was a rustle among the women, and a whisper, "It's Wendell
Phillips." His young wife, Ann, a delegate from the Massachusetts Society, sat near Elizabeth.

What a beautiful voice Mr. Phillips had, and how skill-
fully he chose his words. With a thankful heart Elizabeth
heard him move in ringing tones that "all persons bearing
credentials from any body" be recognized as members of the
convention. He was followed by an Englishman, Dr. John
Bowring, who enthusiastically seconded the motion, urging
the members "to welcome gratefully women to its ranks."

Another Briton at once thundered that it would be better
for the convention to close than to admit females, citing passages from the Bible to prove that God had never intended
any but men to take part in such gatherings.

In return, an American, George Bradburn, announced
that if the Bible sanctioned the subjugation of women, then
it would be well to destroy every Bible in the universe in a
grand bonfire. Elizabeth felt like cheering him.

For hours the controversy raged. Elizabeth sat in tense
fury while men lauded women's domestic virtues and sacred

sphere enshrined in the heart of man and home, claiming
that women should be saved from the burden of their rights!

If she could only part the enveloping curtains and shout
heated rebuttals at the bigoted orators! thought Elizabeth.
Did they not know that their words were an insult? It was
unfair for men to so direct their irony and wit against
women, when they were powerless to reply. How could
Lucretia Mott, with a mind keener than most of the male
speakers, bear to sit in apparent calm? Then she noticed the
Quaker woman's hands. The clasped fingers were rigid, each
bone and tendon visible through the delicate skin.

When James G. Birney rose and formally announced his
agreement with those who would bar women, Elizabeth became livid with anger. Why had she ever been civil to such
a tyrant?

Then Henry began to speak, his words vibrant and clear
even in the women's draped enclosure. Elizabeth's heart beat
rapidly. She hoped she would never get over the thrill that
ran through her whenever she heard his voice. At the same
time she was gripped by anxiety. Henry believed in the
equality of women, she knew. But would his belief be strong
enough for him to oppose publicly a senior delegate from
the same organization, one chosen to lead the Liberty party?

Henry's next sentence fell upon her ears like the sweetest
music. With all his eloquence he urged that women be admitted as delegates.

As he spoke, Elizabeth watched Lucretia's taut fingers
relax. When Henry drew his speech to a close, Lucretia
clapped her hands together in silent applause, giving Elizabeth a special smile.

Despite Henry's oratory, and that of other speakers, the

motion to admit women delegates was defeated. Women should feel honored, they were told, that they were permitted to be present in the hall. It was the first time that females had ever been admitted to a business meeting of the anti-slavery organization.

Furious and bitter, the women left the hall. Elizabeth walked with some of the women delegates to the boarding-house on Queen Street, where she and Henry and Mr. Birney also lodged.

"I've never been so betrayed in my life!" announced one of the women.

"To think that we came all this way—for nothing!" another said.

"It was a real sacrifice for me to leave my husband and children," a third remarked. "I'd never have left home had I known that we would not be allowed to take our rightful places in the convention."

"And when I think how I slaved over the speech I was planning to make," a fourth moaned.

Elizabeth could say little. But she felt as keenly as the delegates the insult to her sex.

That night at the dinner table the women gave vent to their indignation. There was no rule that they could not speak there. A special target was James G. Birney. So uncomfortable was he under their gibes that he found other quarters elsewhere, much to Elizabeth's relief. It was now almost impossible for her to be polite to him.

During the long days of the convention Elizabeth listened with only half her mind to the debates. She took scant pride in the fact that Henry had been made a secretary of the meetings. She was in a constant state of indignation.

One afternoon she was so distressed that she left the convention hall early. As she went out, she was pleased to see Lucretia Mott following.

When they reached the sidewalk, Lucretia said, "What a beautiful day! It's worth all the rain we've had to endure. Let's take a walk and let the sunshine dispel some of our mental clouds."

"Clouds!" Elizabeth expostulated. "My head feels as if a thunderstorm were raging in it. I could not stay there another minute and listen to those conceited men orating. I have never heard anyone so illogical!"

"Thou art right," Lucretia said warmly. "They laud the nobility of their cause in freeing the blacks from slavery, but at the same time they place women in a position that is equally degrading."

"Exactly," Elizabeth agreed. "They say how unfair it is that blacks cannot participate in their own government or the making of its laws. But do they think it unfair that women are denied the same privileges?"

"No," Lucretia said, "men cannot seem to see that by their age-old prejudice they are keeping women in a situation almost as restricted as abject servitude."

Their rapid pace brought them to a park where nurses wheeled rosy-cheeked infants in prams, schoolgirls rolled hoops, and boys played soccer. But neither American woman had eyes for those around them.

"It's intolerable for us to be treated so," Elizabeth said. Suddenly she remembered her mother stirring the ballots before the altar in the Johnstown church. "There must be *something* we can do to lift ourselves out of this abyss."

For a few minutes they walked on. Elizabeth's mind was

in a whirl. All at once she exclaimed, "We should hold a convention for women! We could discuss women's rights, and we could decide upon a course of action."

Her thoughts raced on. "We could list all the things that are wrong in regard to women—that they are denied an equal chance in education or training for business, that they are barred from the professions, that they have few legal rights, and no ability to change the laws."

"Yes," Lucretia said, her voice deep with emotion, "and above all we must prove that women are as capable as men of taking part in the affairs of the world."

She looked deep into Elizabeth's eyes. "Thou hast had an inspiration, Elizabeth Stanton," she said. "After we return to America we must surely hold a convention for women's rights."

10

THE KEY TO POWER

*I*n her new home in Chelsea, a fashionable suburb of Boston, Elizabeth stood before a mirror, smoothing her brown curls and regarding her new gown with satisfaction. The bright blue suited her, matching her eyes and complementing her high color. The broad collar tended to offset the fact that she was five months pregnant.

If only this baby should be a girl, she would be supremely happy. She had certainly done her duty for the male population, having already produced two sons, the first named for her father and the second for Henry. Aged three and one, they were dynamos of energy. It was a relief to have them in their beds napping, as they were now, early on this spring afternoon in 1845.

What a joy it would be to have a daughter whom she could bring up in complete equality with the boys of the family! This would be one girl who would never be barred from interesting pursuits simply because they were not "ladylike." Thank heaven the educational situation had improved somewhat, and some colleges now admitted women.

In other areas, though, a woman's lot was as narrow and restricted as it had been when Elizabeth was a girl. Daily she chafed under the attitude of men, that woman's place was in the home, that it was improper for her to take part in business, to speak in public, or to enter the professions. The laws were still unfair, giving all power to husbands and none to wives, so that married women were virtually at their husband's mercy.

Just a short while ago Lucretia Mott had paid a visit to Boston. What a wonderful reunion they had had at their first meeting since London. And how heatedly Elizabeth and Lucretia had talked about the disadvantages under which women labored! Our sex is not much better off than are slaves, they decided. Someday soon we must call the convention for women's rights that we talked about in London.

All too soon their afternoon together came to an end. Lucretia returned to Philadelphia and her family, and Elizabeth to her babies. But their correspondence flourished.

Into Elizabeth's bedroom floated the rich fragrance of pot roast simmering on the kitchen range. It should be ready by tonight in case she and Henry should bring home guests. She prided herself upon being able to provide for extra appetites at any time upon short notice. It was just a matter of good management.

In fact, the whole business of housekeeping depended simply upon organization. Of course it was a help to have a pump in the back yard and an iron range in the kitchen. Such modern conveniences kept the servants content. Why other women fussed over household details she could not imagine. If one used her head to plan and carry out the necessary steps in maintaining a home, one could have plenty of time for more interesting pursuits.

Today, for instance, she was going to hear the celebrated black orator, Frederick Douglass, speak in Boston. She had gone early to market this morning with Norah, the cook, while Moira, the second maid, tidied the house, and Bassett, the nurse, looked after the boys. On her return she had arranged fresh flowers, written some letters, and read to Neil, the older boy, for a while before lunch.

Tying her bonnet in place, she left the pleasant two-story house and walked down the hill to the Winnisimmet ferry slip. There she took a boat across the harbor to the Hanover Street landing in Boston. The long, double-seated, horse-drawn omnibus was waiting. Should she ride today? No, it was more healthful to walk, especially in her present condition. She had tramped miles when she was carrying the other babies, and they were strong, husky creatures. The walk would be good for her, too. She had heard that women who exercised regularly had easier deliveries. Her first two had been no picnic, but she had not suffered the agonies described by some of her friends.

Elizabeth stepped out briskly, glorying in the fresh spring air, crisp with salt from the nearby Atlantic. How she loved the ocean at this time of year. And how she dreaded the effect of its harsh, raw winds on Henry's throat and lungs in the winter. He had been so ill last February that the doctor had suggested they move away from the sea to an inland location where the air was drier.

The thought of moving away from Boston was dreadful. She would not think about it now. There was so much to look at here on Hanover Street—the new Brick Church designed by Charles Bulfinch, the old North Church two blocks off to the right, the Oyster House on Union Street, Faneuil Hall and the Quincy Market, the old State House, Ticknor's Bookstore, and the old South Meeting House.

Now she had reached Marlborough Chapel on Washington Street, where many controversial subjects were aired. Thankfully she sank into a seat near the front. If Henry could get away from his law practice in time to attend the lecture, he could find her there. She was so short of stature, a fact that plagued her continually, that she could not see much of anything from the back.

Gradually at first, then rapidly, the hall filled. She watched the faces that had become familiar to her, and smiled and nodded to each person in turn. There was Theodore Parker, whose sermon she had listened to here last Sunday with keen approbation, and John Greenleaf Whittier, whom she and Henry had visited recently at his home in Amesbury. There was Ralph Waldo Emerson, with the brow of a dreamer, and Bronson Alcott, looking harassed. Farther on were William Lloyd Garrison and his wife, dedicated souls, if ever there were.

Two years ago Elizabeth and Henry had moved to Boston, where he had been admitted to the Massachusetts Bar after a year of studying law with her father, during which time the two men had grown to accept and like each other. On her arrival in Boston, Elizabeth had known hardly anyone except the delegates to the Anti-Slavery Convention whom she had met in London. But Henry knew everyone, it seemed. And now she herself was acquainted with scores of fascinating, intelligent people.

She had never been exposed to so stimulating an atmosphere as there was here in Boston. No wonder Wendell Phillips called it the "brain of the Union." New ideas were constantly being tossed into the air, discussed, and acted upon.

Where else but near Boston would one find a community such as Brook Farm, where cultured men and women banded together to do their own farming and housework, making time for lectures, reading, music, dancing, and games? After a two-day visit there, Elizabeth could understand how Brook Farm members found isolated homes, by contrast, to be solitary, silent, and selfish.

Where else but in Boston could one attend gatherings such as Margaret Fuller's Conversations or find such a galaxy of intellects gathered to exchange ideas?

Suddenly Elizabeth sat up, all attention, for the program was beginning. Onto the stage filed the Hutchinson family, four handsome, clean-limbed brothers in blue broadcloth and white collars, and their little sister Abby in silk, soft lace, and blue ribbons. Their clear sweet voices seemed to bring all the freshness and beauty of their native New Hampshire into the crowded hall.

A stir went through the audience as Frederick Douglass walked to the podium. Over six feet tall, strong and well-proportioned, he stood as if conscious of his dignity and power, as regal as an African monarch. Could this man have ever been a slave? Incredible, Elizabeth thought.

Then Douglass began to speak. With his words, the walls of the crowded auditorium began to recede. Elizabeth could almost see the plantation that he pictured, the toil, sorrow, and wretched living conditions of the slaves. Then he told of the overseer's lash, manacles, thumb-stringing, and tortures too horrible to contemplate. When he described his flight from the South, fearful at every moment, she felt almost as if she were taking the same perilous journey to freedom in the North.

When Frederick Douglass had finished speaking, Elizabeth sat for a moment as in a trance. What indignities and

cruelties this man and others had suffered! That he had survived to educate himself and win an honored place on the
platform was proof that the color of a man's skin was no in-
dication of his level of intelligence.

Eagerly she joined the queue of people gathering to con-
gratulate the speaker.

When she came up to him, she said, "I am Elizabeth Cady
Stanton. I was deeply impressed by your splendid talk. No
one who heard you can fail to be convinced of the need for
equal opportunity for all."

Mr. Douglass bowed courteously. "Thank you, madam."
Then he looked at her questioningly. "Might I ask if you are
related to Mr. Henry B. Stanton?"

Elizabeth could feel the blood rising to her cheeks. She
could never hear Henry's name without a rush of joy. "He
is my husband," she said proudly.

"Mrs. Stanton, there is something it would give me great
pleasure to tell you if you have time to hear it."

"I do indeed," Elizabeth said. She glanced around at the
crowd that pressed near. "But there are others who are in a
hurry to greet you. I shall wait over there until you are
free." The line of people looked formidably long, and she
was tired, but if this leader of his race had something to tell
her about her dear Henry, she would wait until midnight.
She found a chair nearby and sat down.

A short time later Mr. Douglass approached. "I am sorry
to have kept you waiting," he said, "but I am anxious to discharge in some way a debt I have long owed your husband."

Elizabeth smiled at him. "Won't you be seated?" she
asked, gesturing to the chair beside her.

"You have no objection?" He looked at the people still remaining in the hall.

"To what?" she asked.

"To being seen sitting beside a black man?"

"Mr. Douglass, I would be honored," she said, inwardly pierced by shame that in her country such a situation could exist. "Now please tell me what you have to say about my husband."

"It happened just after I had escaped from the South, and had sought refuge with a friend in the North. I was tired and discouraged and uncertain what to do with my freedom now that I had it. My friend took me to hear Mr. Stanton speak. I had never heard anyone like him." The former slave's eyes filled with tears. "He made me feel that I was indeed a man and that there was nothing in the world I might not do."

Elizabeth smiled mistily. She knew very well Henry's power to move people. Hadn't she herself come under his spell six years ago?

"And so?" she questioned.

"I determined to gain an education and to help my people find freedom and dignity. That is what I am doing today, and shall do, for years to come, God willing."

"Amen," Elizabeth breathed.

"I have told Mr. Stanton how grateful I am to him, and that I consider him the greatest orator in the antislavery movement, but he simply says that he is only one among many. I want you to know, Mrs. Stanton, that if there is ever anything that I can do to help you and Mr. Stanton, I stand ready to do so."

"If a need should arise, you may be sure there is no one to whom we would rather turn for assistance," Elizabeth said.

There was so much she would like to discuss with this man. She spoke next of the subject that was ever uppermost in her mind.

"Tell me, Mr. Douglass, how you feel in regard to the position of women. Do you believe that they should share in the freedom you are striving for?"

"You do not think that I would deny to my mother, my sisters, or any other woman the rights that I ask for myself and other men?" Frederick Douglass demanded. "Indeed, no. I believe that women should have exactly the same rights as men."

"How I wish that others would feel as you do!" Elizabeth said. If only she knew how to go about achieving rights for women. Perhaps this black leader could give her some direction in the steps she should take to better the status of women.

"Mr. Douglass, what do you consider the one most important need of your people in order to gain complete equality?"

For a moment the man was silent. Then he turned to her, his eyes blazing. "Mrs. Stanton, the answer to that is simple. The ballot is the key to power. Before they can take their rightful place in the United States, Negroes must have the right to vote."

Just then Elizabeth heard a familiar, quick step. She turned and saw Henry. Proudly she watched the two men greet each other, respect and admiration plain upon each handsome face.

Henry turned to Elizabeth. "My dear, I'm delighted that you have met Mr. Douglass. You have invited him to dinner, I hope?"

"Not yet, but I do as of this moment. Will you take pot luck with us, sir?"

"You are very kind." The tall man hesitated. "I should be catching a train."

"You can take a later one. Come along with us now." Henry took Frederick Douglass's arm, and together the three left the hall.

Not until the next day did Elizabeth realize that she had taken a radical step. The maids reported that all Chelsea was agog. The Stantons had had a black man as a guest at their home and had sat down to dinner with him! What was the world coming to?

11

THE NINTH RESOLUTION

*T*hou art looking well, Elizabeth," Lucretia Mott said in her clear, sweet voice, smiling over her teacup on the afternoon of July 13, 1848, in the parlor of the Hunt mansion in Waterloo, New York. She and Elizabeth sat beside a small table with three other married women—their hostess, Jane C. Hunt; her neighbor, Mary Ann McClintock; and Lucretia's sister, Martha C. Wright, at whose home Lucretia and James Mott were visiting for a few days.

"I'm glad that you think so," Elizabeth said, laughing ruefully. It seemed to her that her life had been one crisis after another since she and Henry had moved to Seneca Falls, New York, two years ago. First she had superintended the repair and renovation of the house they occupied, which was owned by her father. Then she had nursed her sons through various childhood illnesses. When they were well she must constantly be on the alert lest they fall into the nearby Seneca River or canal. The third baby, born in Chelsea, had been another boy, and was named Gerrit. She loved him dearly, but still longed for a daughter.

Elizabeth had trained a succession of green servant girls, only to lose them to the blandishments of newly arrived, blarneying immigrants. She had welcomed an endless round of guests, not the least of whom were the runaway slaves to whom she gave food and a safe place to sleep on their journey to freedom in Canada. She had taken bundles of food

and clothing to needy families on the flats beside the river at
the foot of the bluff below her home, had listened to their
troubles, and had tried to help them, often called upon to
make a judgment in their heated disputes.

During Henry's frequent absences, when he was called
away on business from his law office or to speak at temperance or antislavery meetings, Elizabeth felt trapped by her
myriad responsibilities. In Boston she had never dreamed
that she would ever be so burdened. It seemed unfair that
women should have to be wives, mothers, housekeepers,
physicians, and spiritual guides, while men were free to deal
with government and reform. If Emerson's statement was
true that "A healthy discontent is the first step to progress,"
she was certainly ready for that step! But how should she go
about remedying the wrongs of society in general and of
women in particular and still be a good wife and mother?

"Is thy husband's health better here than in Boston?" Lucretia asked.

"Much better," Elizabeth answered. "The dry air is very
beneficial to his lungs." It was on the tip of her tongue to
blurt out how keenly she missed Boston and its stimulating
atmosphere, to say nothing of the well-trained servants who
had looked after her house and children so that she could
often go out to concerts and meetings. But she had no wish
to hurt the feelings of these Quaker women, the most liberal
thinkers she had met in the area.

"My next-door neighbor's husband just died of consump-
tion," Mrs. McClintock remarked. "His illness used up their
savings, and now she has to support her five children."

"How is she going to manage?" Mrs. Wright asked.

"Take in boarders, or do dressmaking, probably. She used

to keep all the accounts for her husband's business, but no one will hire a woman as bookkeeper."

"It's the same old story. Men refuse to let women take part in anything that requires intelligence," Mrs. Hunt said bitterly.

"Or pays a good salary!" Mrs. McClintock sputtered.

"Hast thou read Margaret Fuller's essay 'The Great Law-Suit'?" Lucretia inquired. "She argues well for equality in education, industry, and politics."

"Or the Reverend Samuel May's sermon that he gave three years ago in Syracuse on the rights and conditions of women?" Martha Wright added.

"Or Lydia Maria Child's *Fact and Fiction*?" Jane Hunt asked. "She certainly tells how terribly women have suffered under men's laws."

"At least the lawmakers have taken one positive step to improve our status," Elizabeth said. "Thank goodness for the passage this spring of the married woman's property bill."

"Amen to that," Mrs. McClintock said. "Now a woman can hold real estate in her own name. What a blessing that will be to thousands of wives."

Elizabeth warmed with a glow of personal satisfaction. During visits to her parents in Albany, where the Cady family in recent years occasionally made extended stays, she had talked to legislators, urging the passage of the bill.

Suddenly she had an inspiration. "Talking among ourselves isn't going to do a bit of good," she declared. "It's time we took some action."

"What can we do?" Mrs. McClintock asked.

"We can hold a convention. Don't you remember, Lucretia? You and I talked about it in London when we were so furious over women delegates being barred from the Anti-Slavery proceedings. And when you visited in Boston, we said that soon we should hold a convention for woman's rights!" Elizabeth cried in excitement.

"I remember it well," Lucretia said, her eyes sparkling.

"Do you think anyone would come?" Mrs. Hunt asked uncertainly.

"Of course they would. If I heard about such a meeting, wild horses couldn't keep me away," Mrs. McClintock declared.

"What do you think, Lucretia?" Martha Wright asked.

"If men can hold conventions to stir up people and effect reform, I see no reason why women should not use the same means," the Quaker woman said with quiet authority. "The first thing to do is to put a notice in the paper."

The next morning the group met again. Elizabeth's eye raced over the columns of the *Seneca County Courier*, past advertisements for new parasols just received by railroad, Dr. Phelph's Compound Tomato Pills, a Live Mammoth Crocodile to be seen on the canal boat *Rome*, and a lost bead bag containing a three-dollar bill. Ah, there was the paragraph she had helped compose. Triumphantly she read it aloud.

SENECA FALLS CONVENTION
WOMAN'S RIGHTS CONVENTION.—A Convention to discuss the social, civil, and religious condition and rights of woman will be held in the Wesleyan Chapel, at Seneca Falls, N.Y., on Wednesday and Thursday, the 19th and 20th of July, current; commencing at 10 o'clock A.M. During the first day the meeting will be exclusively for women, who are earnestly

invited to attend. The public generally are invited to be present
on the second day, when Lucretia Mott, of Philadelphia, and
other ladies and gentlemen, will address the convention.

As Elizabeth read, she realized that today was July 14,
Bastille Day. If only the bastions of male supremacy would
fall as dramatically as had the famous French prison!

The next moment she was gripped by crushing responsibility as Lucretia Mott said impressively, "You realize, ladies, that we have less than a week in which to prepare for a
convention that will occupy two days. Many organizations
take an entire year making up a program of similar length.
We must not waste a moment. Now, how shall we organize
our points?"

"I've been looking over these reports of peace and temperance and antislavery conventions, but they all seem too
tame," Elizabeth said, holding up a sheaf of printed sheets.
"We need a new and original program for a rebellion such
as ours."

"But it must be dignified if it's to command the respect it
deserves," Lucretia insisted. "Suppose we begin by listing
the wrongs we hope to correct."

Into Elizabeth's mind flashed the memory of the recent
Fourth of July celebration to which she and Henry had
taken the two older boys, now six and four. One of the main
features, customary in every town of the United States, was
the ceremonious public reading of the Declaration of Independence.

"Let's write a Declaration of Woman's Independence,"
Elizabeth suggested.

"That sounds too radical," Mrs. Hunt objected.

"How about calling it a Declaration of Sentiments, then?" Elizabeth asked, borrowing a title known to them all from the first national antislavery convention of 1833. "We can still use the Declaration of Independence as our model— like this: 'We hold these truths to be self-evident: that all men *and women* are created equal.' "

The group took up the idea eagerly, using statute books, church usages, and social customs as sources for a list of grievances, eighteen in all, the same number as in the Declaration of 1776.

When they had finished, Elizabeth read the draft aloud in triumph: "The history of mankind is a history of repeated injuries and usurpations on the part of man toward woman, having in direct object the establishment of an absolute tyranny over her. . . .

"He has never permitted her to exercise her inalienable right to the elective franchise.

"He has compelled her to submit to laws, in the formation of which she had no voice.

"He has withheld from her rights which are given to the most ignorant and degraded men—both natives and foreigners.

"Having deprived her of this first right of a citizen, the elective franchise, thereby leaving her without representation in the halls of legislation, he has oppressed her on all sides.

"He has made her, if married, in the eye of the law, civilly dead.

"He has taken from her all right in property, even to the wages she earns.

"In the covenant of marriage, she is compelled to promise

obedience to her husband . . ." Elizabeth paused a moment. Thank heaven she had insisted that the word *obey* be deleted from her wedding ceremony. In a strong voice she continued reading, "he becoming . . . her master—the law giving him power to deprive her of her liberty, and to administer chastisement.

"He has so framed the laws of divorce as to be wholly regardless of the happiness of women. . . .

"He has taxed her to support a government which recognizes her only when her property can be made profitable to it. . . .

"He closes against her all the avenues to wealth and distinction, which he considers most honorable to himself. As a teacher of theology, medicine, or law, she is not known.

"He has denied her the facilities for obtaining a thorough education.

"He allows her in Church, as well as State, but a subordinate position. . . .

"He has created a false public sentiment by giving to the world a different code of morals for men and women, by which moral delinquencies which exclude women from society, are . . . deemed of little account in man.

"He has . . . assigned for her a sphere of action, when that belongs to her conscience and to her God.

"He has endeavored . . . to destroy her confidence in her own powers, to lessen her self-respect, and to make her willing to lead a dependent and abject life."

They were all there, Elizabeth thought with satisfaction, all the wrongs that she had bitterly resented from her childhood days. Then she had seen them only as they affected other women. Now she herself was experiencing and smarting under many of those tyrannous rules. They must be overthrown. Women must gain the place they deserved— on an equal footing with men. If Elizabeth should do nothing else in her lifetime, she would work for that equality. Oh, how she would work for it!

In a later meeting the group decided that they must form a set of resolutions to implement their ideas.

"Resolved," said one, "that all laws which prevent woman from occupying such a station in society as her conscience shall dictate, or which place her in a position inferior to that of man, are contrary to the great precept of nature, and therefore of no force or authority."

"Resolved," said another, "that woman is man's equal— was intended to be so by the Creator, and the highest good of the race demands that she should be recognized as such."

As she listened to the sincere voices around her, Elizabeth decided that here was the proper place to demand votes for women. Without a voice in lawmaking, women would be powerless to effect any change in their status.

Words began to form in her mind. *Resolved: that the women of this country must demand the right to vote.* No, that was too weak. She must strengthen her statement, make it so strong that it could not fail to stir women deeply.

How could she best appeal to responsible women? Through their sense of duty. Very well then, Elizabeth would put that in. *Resolved: that it is the duty of the women of this country to—* What word next? *Demand* was too weak; it left the work unfinished. There must be a stronger word or words. Ah, she had it—*secure to themselves.*

Now, next—the right to vote? No, that was too abrupt. Frantically she fought for words, then stopped in triumph. She would include the word *sacred*. Everyone respected that term. And she would use *elective franchise* since it had a more authoritative ring than the word *vote*.

As the secretary paused in her writing, Elizabeth said, "I have thought of the Ninth Resolution. It is really the foundation of them all. Without it we can accomplish nothing." Then in a firm voice she said, *"Resolved: that it is the duty of the women of this country to secure to themselves their sacred right to the elective franchise."*

Flushed with triumph, Elizabeth waited. There was a dead silence. Then Lucretia Mott bent her serious gaze upon Elizabeth and said, "If thou demands that, thou will make us ridiculous. We must go slowly."

Stunned, Elizabeth looked at Lucretia in wordless astonishment. How could Lucretia, of all women, hesitate over this demand? Lucretia, whose intelligence and judgment Elizabeth admired above all women's!

Others of the group demurred. "It might be better to wait until a more propitious time," Mrs. Hunt suggested. "Why arouse antagonism needlessly?"

"Needlessly?" Elizabeth almost screamed her question. "Two of our grievances are concerned with women's lack of the elective franchise. Don't you think that there is a real need for women to have a hand in the making of laws? How else can we combat such evils as men's complete command over us and our children? How else can we gain access to our proper sphere of absolute equality with men?"

At length, half-heartedly, the others consented. They would include the Ninth Resolution. Whether it would be adopted would depend upon the vote of the convention.

12

HER SACRED RIGHT

*N*ever in all her life had she felt quite so terrifyingly alone, thought Elizabeth. Not in the boatswain's chair at the top of the ship's mast swinging far out over the vast Atlantic. Not even in the agony of childbirth. Then the infant she was struggling to bring into the world belonged to Henry, too. This child of her mind—the demand for woman's enfranchisement—was her own creation. She and she alone was its sole progenitor, and upon her efforts depended its very life.

When, racked with pain, she had delivered her first-born, Henry had been nearby, his love sustaining and strengthening her. Today Henry was far away, off on some trumped-up business in another part of the county, carrying out his threat to leave town if she persisted in her ridiculous demand. She was upheld only by her courage and the conviction that her resolution presented the one logical means by which women might gain their rightful place in the universe.

How heatedly she and Henry had argued two nights ago when she had read him the Ninth Resolution. The very idea of women voting was so new, so revolutionary, so contrary to established custom that Henry had opposed it vehemently. Above all, he objected to *his wife* publicly making such a demand.

In vain Elizabeth had attempted logic, citing the orderly

points that were usually the only way to reach his legally trained mind. In vain she had pointed out that Henry, as a reasonable man and courageous abolitionist, should perceive the clear connection between woman's position and that of the slave. Couldn't he see that only the complete novelty of her resolution aroused his ire? If he would just take time to get used to the idea, she pleaded, and would sleep on it, by tomorrow morning he could not fail to accept her premise as sound.

But when the new day came, Henry had been as obdurate as the night before. And so had she. Head high, determination unwavering, she had stood in the doorway watching him drive off in the carriage. And he, every line of his long, lean body stiff with indignant self-righteousness, had brought the reins down over the horse's back with a re-sounding *whupp*, as if to emphasize the inviolability of his stand.

So here she was, sitting in outward composure on the platform of the Wesleyan Chapel in Seneca Falls this twentieth day of July with other members of the First Woman's Rights Convention. Inwardly she was in turmoil.

If only someone from among her family or close friends were in agreement with her resolution, she might not feel so alone. But in the entire assemblage just one person, to her certain knowledge, wholly approved of the demand she was about to make. She had a tremendous respect for Frederick Douglass and was deeply grateful for his support in this instance. But even with all his fame and high repute could he, a former slave, convince people of the necessity for woman's enfranchisement?

How she wished that she were tall and commanding or

that she had the advantage of age! Her plump, rosy cheeks, round blue eyes, and soft brown curls made her appear younger than her thirty-two years. It was difficult to convince people that she was qualified by study and discussion to point the way out of the unjust civil and legal limitations that kept women in a state little better than slavery.

Suddenly she stiffened and peered toward the back of the hall. A tall, angular man was entering. Had Henry repented of his decision and returned in time to hear her speak? No, the man was a stranger. Her heart sank. Then hope revived. Perhaps Henry had slipped in without her noticing. She would study every row of the crowded chapel on the chance of finding him.

As on the day before, the audience was composed chiefly of women, some young, some old, but all asimmer with excitement at this pioneer gathering to air and act upon the grievances of women. Faces flushed with the summer heat, they sat erect in their tight-waisted dresses, twitching their long skirts into place as newcomers sidled into the few remaining seats.

Here and there sat a sparse scattering of men, grouped as if requiring the company of their fellows in so largely feminine a gathering. A few seemed willing to listen to what the female sex might have to say. More had an air of gleeful expectancy, as if waiting for some statement upon which they might cast the full weight of their lordly derision.

As her gaze slid over the last seat of the last row, Elizabeth realized with a pang that Henry had not come. If only he had reconsidered his stand and ignored the dire possibilities he had predicted should he attend the meeting. His position as an attorney would surely be impaired, he had said. His reputation as an antislavery speaker would be injured. His political future would be irreparably damaged. Didn't she realize, he had thundered, that his mere presence would indicate tacit approval of his wife's unprecedented and revolutionary demand? People would think he was actually in favor of her brazen affront to the established order.

On the platform the heat was becoming oppressive. Elizabeth's handkerchief was a damp wad from the perspiration of her palms and brow. Unrolling the sheets of paper covered with her cursive handwriting, she straightened them with trembling fingertips.

A stir went through the audience as James Mott rose, tall, spare, and dignified, the very embodiment of Quaker principles. How fortunate Lucretia was to have a husband who stood by her in every cause, thought Elizabeth. She fastened her eyes upon his straight back in its plain coat. As she listened to his calm voice, her panic lessened.

One by one the women speakers rose, offering the various resolutions prepared—that woman is man's equal, that she should be encouraged to develop her intellect, speak in public, and move out into an enlarged sphere of activity. One by one the resolutions were discussed and voted upon with approval.

Then James Mott turned from his place at the podium. He gestured toward her and said, "I now present Mrs. Elizabeth Cady Stanton, who will read the Ninth Resolution."

All at once she was on her feet, moving to the center of the platform, her heart pounding. She could not falter now.

"*Resolved*," she proclaimed, her voice clear and ringing,

"that it is the duty of the women of this country to secure to themselves their sacred right to the elective franchise."

As she finished, she could feel the blood rushing to her cheeks, the tears ready to start from her eyes. In the silence that followed, she waited, hardly able to breathe.

There was a muttering in various parts of the hall as people said, "The franchise—she must mean the right to vote."

Then, like a wave breaking, there rose a babble of voices.

"Women—vote? Who ever heard of such a thing?"

"Ladies go to the polls?"

"The ballot in the hands of women? Might as well turn the world upside down!"

Incredulously Elizabeth listened. She should have realized that her resolution would stir up a hornet's nest, and that many of her own sex would be among those expressing amazement and scorn for the idea.

But what utter folly for all women not to stand behind her. Could they not understand that by the ballot, and the ballot alone, women would take their rightful and responsible place in the world? She must convince them of the essential soundness of the move, its inevitable rightness as a first step toward equality of the sexes.

With relief she saw Frederick Douglass rise to his impressive height, his handsome black features composed. How princelike was his dignity. The crowd could not help but be swayed by his appeal. Many of them knew him now that he was a respected citizen of Rochester, the editor and publisher of the *North Star*. Gratefully she listened to his remarks, noting with approval each argument he brought forward.

Then Elizabeth began her speech. Since the laws of the United States constituted bars to woman's freedom, she said, only by changing those laws could woman better her condition. In order to change laws, woman must be able to cast her vote for legislators who would make new laws to improve the status of woman. Therefore woman must have the right to vote. It was as simple as that.

Amid a scattering of applause, she sank down upon her chair. Her resolution had indeed created a sensation. But had it any chance of being approved?

Now other speakers rose to voice their protest against so radical a proposal. God had set the bounds of woman's sphere, and she should be satisfied with her position, some said.

Elizabeth felt the icy grip of doubt. Had she been premature in her demand? Should she have listened to Jane Hunt and waited for a more propitious time?

Then James Mott was calling for a vote. In silent agony Elizabeth tried to count the hands upraised in favor, then those lifted in oppositon. The scene swam before her eyes. She was too agitated. She would have to wait for the official word. There was a long pause while the tellers conferred.

At length the moderator pounded with his gavel. "Resolution number Nine," he announced, "has passed."

Elizabeth hardly heard the speaker presenting the Tenth Resolution. Her heart was nearly bursting. Her resolution had passed! The convention had approved the idea of votes for women!

Reason warned that this decision was only a first step toward woman suffrage. There would be disappointments ahead, and much hard work, to convince men, and women too, that in the vote lay the salvation of women, the only effective means of lifting themselves out of their present subservient position.

The action of this convention today might be only one step. But it was a step in the right direction. Someday, Elizabeth knew in her heart of hearts, the legislative bodies of the United States must recognize the right of women to take part in the governing of the country.

Surely that day of freedom could not be far off.

Late that evening, when Henry returned, Elizabeth was waiting for him in the sitting room. As the door swung shut behind him, he stepped into the circle of light from the oil lamp on the center table. Elizabeth looked up.

"I trust you had a successful business trip," she said, trying to sound cool and composed.

He bowed. "And I have already heard reports of your so-called convention. Two men in a buggy stopped me ten miles the other side of town to tell me about your demand for votes for women. They could hardly speak for laughing!" Henry's voice was icy.

"It's no laughing matter!" Elizabeth stormed. How could men be so base as to ridicule this necessary reform?

"It certainly is nothing to laugh about," Henry said. "How do you think I feel having men hee-hawing about *my wife?*"

"I hope you told them how important it is that women gain the right to vote," Elizabeth said vehemently.

"I? Tell them that? You know what I think. It's the craziest idea I ever heard of. Women don't know enough about government to have the ballot." Henry towered over her, his eyes glittering beneath his jutting brows.

Elizabeth tilted her head back to look up at him. If she lost her temper now she'd never get anywhere.

"And why don't women know enough?" she challenged. "Who keeps them out of universities and business and professions where they might learn something? The only time they have any contact with the government is when they pay taxes. And that's taxation without representation."

"Women are represented at the polls by their husbands, who vote in the best interests of the women," Henry said.

Elizabeth could feel her fury rising. Why couldn't she cite the arguments she had employed in her speech this afternoon? Why should Henry have the power to enrage her as no stranger possibly could?

"You forget that all women are not wives," she said. "What about the spinsters, the widows, and the divorced? Surely they should have a voice in the making of laws that govern them, although they have not the good fortune to have husbands as their agents in elections." She spat out the words furiously.

"Ah, I'm glad to hear you talking sensibly at last," Henry said loftily. "At least you appreciate your fortunate position as a wife."

Henry's superiority was infuriating. Elizabeth rose and stamped her foot. "I'm not going to demean myself by arguing with you another minute," she said. "Women should have a voice in government, just as men do. We are all created equal, and it's time men realized it and stopped taking advantage of us."

"Taking advantage!" Henry thundered. His face was very red. "Is that the thanks we get for protecting you women?"

"We don't want to be protected," Elizabeth cried. "We want to be free!"

Then, suddenly, completely without warning, she burst into tears. The past week had been more of a strain than she had realized. She had worked late night after night on her speech. Even after going to bed she had lain awake, going over and over each carefully written word in her mind.

The afternoon's ordeal had left her limp, and she had returned home to a household in bedlam, which had required all her efforts to restore to order and harmony.

Blinded by her tears, she all at once felt Henry's strong arms around her, and his face pressed against hers.

"Ah, Elizabeth," he said, "if you only knew how beautiful you are when you lose your temper."

Still furious, she struggled to loose his hold. "How can you talk like that when I'm deadly serious?" she demanded.

"Because I'm serious, too," he said. "I hadn't known until now how much this matter of the vote means to you." Tenderly he touched a teardrop on her cheek. "I'm beginning to see things differently. There's a strong possibility that you may be right. The only sure way women will have the power to change the laws that hamper and restrict them is by having a voice in the formation of reform measures."

Elizabeth listened incredulously. Could this be the same man who two minutes ago was deriding the whole idea of votes for women?

Angrily she brushed her hand across her eyes. She knew and despised women who used tears to accomplish what reason would not. How humiliating that her involuntary weeping had been the pivotal power to change Henry's thinking! Why, oh, why had her feminine weakness been the force that brought him over to her point of view? Why not a stunning argument, a brilliant point of logic?

Gradually she relaxed. No matter how or why. Henry was in agreement with her now. That was all that mattered. Thankfully she leaned her head against his chest.

"Oh, Henry dear, I knew you'd see the logic of it," she said.

13

FOES AND FRIENDS

*F*or a few days the Stanton household was as peaceful as could be expected for a home in which three lively young boys constantly tried out new ways to employ their energy. Elizabeth attempted to compensate for the previous week's neglect by cooking special treats and reading endless stories to the boys.

On August 4, 1848, the *Seneca County Courier* published the resolutions passed at the Woman's Rights Convention. Elizabeth cut out the notice and made plans to attend a similar meeting in Rochester early in August.

A few evenings later, Henry came home bearing a sheaf of articles. Newspapers across the country had picked up the convention report, hailing it with headlines such as PETTICOATS VS. BOOTS, INSURRECTION AMONG WOMEN, and THE REIGN OF PETTICOATS. The meeting itself had received little attention. It was Elizabeth's Ninth Resolution that aroused rage, ridicule, and in a few rare instances—admiration.

"It appears, my dear," Henry commented, "that you have a tiger by the tail!"

Some of the articles left Elizabeth speechless with fury, such as the *Philadelphia Public Ledger's*: *A woman is nobody, A wife is everything. A pretty girl is equal to ten thousand men, and a mother is, next to god, all powerful. . . . The ladies of Philadelphia, therefore, under the influence of the most sober, serious, second thoughts are resolved to maintain their rights as Wives, Belles, Virgins, and Mothers, and not as Women.*

Elizabeth clenched her fists. "Just wait until Lucretia sees that mess of sentimental claptrap!" she stormed.

"Before you read any others, look at what Horace Greeley has to say in the *New York Tribune*," Henry said, putting a news sheet into her hand.

Elizabeth looked up in amazement. "Horace Greeley?" she asked. "Do you mean to say that *he* has mentioned woman's rights in his paper?"

"Not only mentioned it, but devoted an entire editorial to it," Henry replied. The pride in his voice was unmistakable. Elizabeth barely controlled a smile. Was this the same Henry who a short time ago had vigorously opposed her demand?

Gratefully she read from the *Tribune: It is easy to be smart, to be droll, to be facetious in opposition to the demands of these Female Reformers; and in decrying assumptions so novel and opposed to established habits and usages, a little wit will go a great way. But when a sincere republican is asked to say in sober earnest what adequate reason he can give for refusing the demand of woman to an equal participation with men in political rights, he must answer, None at all.*

Elizabeth waved the paper in the air. "Good for Mr. Greeley!" she cried. Then she read on: *True, he may say the great majority desire no such thing; that they prefer to devote their time to the discharge of home duties, etc. . . . . However unwise and mistaken the demand, it is but the assertion of a natural right and as such must be conceded.*

If only he had not tacked on those weakening statements.

"How does Horace Greeley presume to understand how the great majority of women feel?" Elizabeth demanded. "Little he knows about home duties! And where does he get the authority to judge our demand as unwise and mistaken?"

"Don't be too critical, Liz," Henry warned. "Basically, Greeley is on our side."

Our side. What a happy ring those words had.

Elizabeth threw her arms around Henry. "I wish all men had your viewpoint."

"They're not all lucky enough to have someone like you to set them on the right track," Henry said wryly.

"Perhaps if I wrote, very tactfully, pointing out just why women need the vote, Mr. Greeley might print my letter," Elizabeth said.

That evening, after the boys were safely tucked into bed and Henry was busy with a client, Elizabeth sat at her desk, her pen racing over the page. This letter to Horace Greeley must be well thought out and well written if it were to do its work.

Almost overnight Elizabeth felt a change come over her. Since moving to Seneca Falls she had been wearied and worn out by domestic details, too tired to entertain, too discouraged to make the trip to town except when absolutely necessary, almost too fatigued to read.

Suddenly she found the days too short for all she wished to accomplish. For the first time since her school days she was exercising her mental powers to their utmost, reading omnivorously, evolving new arguments to strengthen her belief, and writing to individuals and newspapers far and wide in support of her theories.

She flew through duties that had previously taken tedious

hours. She filled the house with guests. She attended an end-less number of meetings. And whenever she could, she went to her desk and wrote. It seemed that her pen was forever skimming over the page, setting down ideas for the emanci-pation of women, the need for them to enter business, the advantage of coeducation, and the necessity of new and just laws in relation to married women.

Marveling at her new found energy, Elizabeth rejoiced that she had at last found her life's goal. From now on, she determined, she would pour all her strength, all her effort, and whatever talent she possessed into the one cause that for her was paramount—the enfranchisement of woman!

Her resolve was soon put to the test.

Soon Elizabeth was invited to speak at the nearby town of Junius, and, for the first time, she was offered a fee of ten dollars. She went to work on her speech, and was progres-sing well when she received word that her father would pay her a visit—on the day before her scheduled talk.

Elizabeth set about readying the house, and planned a gala dinner for the evening of his arrival. A year ago Daniel Cady had been elected a Judge of the New York Supreme Court, an honor long overdue, it was said.

When Judge Cady walked into the Stanton house, he had eyes only for Elizabeth. She could see concern written in every line of his face.

"Are you quite well, daughter?" he inquired anxiously. "After seeing your activities written up in the newspapers, I began to think your mind might be deranged."

"Of course I am all right," Elizabeth assured him. "I have never felt more sane in my life."

All during dinner she could feel his concern. Later in the

evening they sat together in the parlor. Henry had sensed
their need to be alone and had retired to his study.

"I understand that you plan to give a speech tomorrow in
Junius," the Judge said. "What do you intend to say?"

"I'll read it to you," Elizabeth offered. Surely, after he
heard her well-chosen and carefully thought out arguments,
he would see that her mind was as well balanced as ever.

The moment she began to speak, she was shaken by em-
barrassment. It was easier to confront a group of strangers
than the father whom she adored, hoped to please, and often
antagonized. With a shaking voice she told of woman's desperate need for a part in making the laws that governed her.

As she concluded, Judge Cady said sternly, "Elizabeth, I
advise you not to give that speech tomorrow. You have already aroused unpleasant publicity, and have made yourself
a target of ridicule. If you persist in going on the platform,
you will become a laughingstock."

How could Father, in whose office she had first learned of
the wrongs perpetrated against women, not understand her
feeling? For all his intelligence, he was as insensitive as other
men to woman's need for equal responsibility in civil and
political affairs.

"But I believe in all that I have said. I cannot remain silent. I must tell other women how they can free themselves
from their present bondage."

"Bondage—humph! You are talking about laws that
give necessary protection to women," the judge thundered.

Now it was Elizabeth's turn to flare up. "Do you call it
protection when men deny women the inalienable rights
listed in the Declaration of Independence?"

"Are you referring to the bona fide document," Daniel Cady asked, "or that traversty you and those other women composed?"

Elizabeth bit her lip, struggling for self-control. She must be calm; she must argue logically. Otherwise she would never convince him of the absolute right of her cause.

But although she marshaled all her facts, she could not move her parent one inch. And despite his urging, she refused to give in to his demand that she cancel her speech.

Finally, after midnight, he delivered an ultimatum. "If you persist in speaking tomorrow, it will be the most costly act of your life!"

Costly act? That could mean only one thing. Her father would disinherit her. For a brief moment Elizabeth hesitated. Her share in his estate would be considerable, for he was a very wealthy man. But what was money compared with her duty to women everywhere? She could not live with herself if she should abandon the cause of women's rights.

Mentally she repeated to herself: *It is the duty of the women of this country to secure for themselves their sacred right to the elective franchise.* Fortified, she faced her father.

"Nothing that you can say will make me change my mind," she said.

Tight-lipped, the judge picked up his bedtime candle and marched out one door. Equally tight-lipped, Elizabeth picked up her candle and departed through another door.

As she climbed the stairs to her bedroom, part of her was furious that her father should be so blind to the needs of women. Another part of her yearned to make peace with him. How difficult it was to blaze new pathways. And why had this major disagreement occurred on just this evening, when she should have been reviewing her speech? Angry and upset, she tossed for hours.

The following day Judge Cady departed—chill, withdrawn, and disapproving.

And on that same day Elizabeth went to Junius and gave her talk—weary, nervous, and dedicated.

From then on Elizabeth redoubled her efforts for woman's rights. She wrote papers to be read at conventions too far away for her to attend. She corresponded widely with individuals about woman's rights. And she continued to write for news columns.

Every word that appeared in print about woman's rights delighted Elizabeth. She wrote to Lucretia, *It will start women thinking, and men, too; and when men and women think about a new question, the first step in progress is taken.*

How thrilled she was to receive a note from Lucretia a few days later: *I am now trying to awaken sufficient interest to hold a woman's rights meeting in this city. . . . Few, however, are accustomed to public speaking. Why can't thou come on here to attend such a meeting? Thou art so wedded to this cause that thou must expect to act as a pioneer in the work.*

For Elizabeth the trip to Philadelphia was an inspiration and encouragement. The meeting was well attended; she met many people in Lucretia's home who believed in woman's rights. And when she returned to Seneca Falls, the children and Henry seemed dearer than ever.

Although the responsibilities of home and children kept her in Seneca Falls most of the time, Elizabeth felt that through her efforts she was joining a worldwide movement toward greater freedom for all individuals. While she went about her household duties, planning meals, taking her children to the dentist, mending their clothes, her active mind was formulating arguments in favor of women's participation in government and business, which she jotted down on whatever scraps of paper came to hand, later incorporating them in her writings.

The more she thought and wrote upon the subject of woman's rights, the more keenly she could see the injustice of the present laws and customs, and the more lucidly she was able to present her thoughts. She continued to speak at public meetings and to answer questions from the platform. It was not always easy, however. To a friend she wrote, *It does seem that this question* [of woman's rights] *will never be perfectly clear to me so that I can answer all the arguments. I often start off quite ably, when lo, I am asked some question I cannot answer. Still hope sustains me, and I read and think as opportunity offers.*

More than hope alone sustained Elizabeth. She had the companionship of other women who became ardent workers for the cause of woman's emancipation.

In Seneca Falls a neighbor and close associate was Mrs. Amelia Bloomer, small and auburn-haired, who edited and published *The Lily*, a temperance paper for women, and who also served as deputy postmaster. Her husband was postmaster, and editor of the *Seneca County Courier*. Amelia's activities in areas traditionally reserved for men made her for a time the laughingstock of the town, but her determination and courage soon convinced people that a woman could capably carry out such work.

Elizabeth became a regular contributor to *The Lily*, at first writing under pseudonyms such as Sunflower or Senex on temperance, coeducation, and above all, woman's rights.

Another staunch ally was her cousin, Libby Smith Miller. Perhaps inspired by her father's contention that so long as women wore clothes that crippled and handicapped them, they would remain in a state of slavery, she developed a new style of dress, a short skirt over a pair of trousers, which allowed far more freedom of movement than the traditional long, voluminous skirt.

When Libby wore her revolutionary new outfit to Seneca Falls, Amelia Bloomer made a similar suit for herself, finding it just the thing to wear when tugging heavy mail sacks into the post office. She praised its advantages so enthusiastically in *The Lily* that readers mistakenly assumed she was its originator, and dubbed it the Bloomer costume. The public in general ridiculed those who adopted the new style, making their lives so miserable that many went back to the old cumbersome skirts. Other courageous souls who put comfort above conformity wore the bloomer in private and in public despite derisive comments.

But Elizabeth could only thank goodness for her new costume. She need not worry about stepping on her hem, or tripping over a ruffle. It was marvelous to be so free, to stride along the street without hampering draperies bunched about her ankles. What a mercy that Libby had had the courage to design and wear the costume! Of course, people would stare and make remarks, but the freedom of being able to walk upstairs carrying a baby and a lighted candle at the same time was worth all the catcalls and howls of laughter.

Elizabeth had cut off not only her skirts, but her long tresses as well. Now she wore her curly hair cropped short. The new style was becoming, she knew. It was wonderful to be a modern woman in the mid-nineteenth century, casting off old restrictions, one by one. There was no telling what far-flung advances women would make once they achieved the right to vote!

One afternoon in 1851 Elizabeth was hurrying home from an antislavery meeting to see that all was in readiness for the dinner party honoring the speakers, William Lloyd Garrison, Henry's old friend and associate, and William Thompson, the noted English abolitionist.

Walking rapidly along Seneca Fall's main thoroughfare, Elizabeth saw two feminine figures standing on a street corner. One, with a crown of auburn curls, was Amelia Bloomer, in a costume similar to her own. Who was Amelia's tall, slender companion? Her long gray gown and bonnet were Quakerlike in their simplicity, though trimmed with ribbons of pale blue.

In a few seconds Elizabeth had reached the corner, and Amelia was saying, "Mrs. Stanton, may I present an earnest worker in the temperance movement, Miss Susan B. Anthony of Rochester?"

Elizabeth clasped strong, slender fingers, and looked up into a face aglow with purpose. The features were plain; one eye had a cast; but the glance that met hers burned with zeal. Innate goodness and steadfastness lent the young woman an air of austere beauty.

"I have been looking forward to meeting you ever since my parents told me how capably you spoke for woman's enfranchisement in Rochester three years ago," Miss Anthony said.

"Do you believe that our sex should be given the ballot?" Elizabeth asked with her usual directness.

"I'd welcome an opportunity to discuss the subject with you," Miss Anthony replied eagerly.

"It would be a pleasure," Elizabeth said. "Can you and Mrs. Bloomer come to call tomorrow afternoon?"

At the others' assent, she hurried on. She had hardly gone a block before she exclaimed in annoyance, "Oh, dear, why didn't I think to invite them for dinner tonight?" She looked back over her shoulder, but the two women were no longer in sight. Elizabeth hurried on, hardly hearing a group of small boys shouting

> Heigh! ho! the carrion crow
> Mrs. Stanton's all the go:
> Twenty tailors take the stitches,
> Mrs. Stanton wears the breeches.

The next day Miss Anthony came to call. Soon she and Elizabeth were deep in discussion. Susan had grown up in a liberal Quaker family where she was encouraged to think for herself and express her ideas. She had taught school for several years, then had thrown her energies into the temperance cause, working to form women's societies to combat alcohol and its attendant evils. From her family's home near Rochester she made frequent trips to surrounding areas to recruit membership and support for the Daughters of Temperance.

"The work you are doing is highly commendable," Elizabeth said. "But don't you see that women can make no real progress in any reform until they secure the ballot? Only by taking part in the legislative process will we be able to change our country's laws."

"You may be right, Mrs. Stanton, but my work now is in the formation of women's societies for temperance. I'd like to do the same for peace and the abolition of slavery, if I could."

"Those are exactly the causes that I feel are of paramount importance," Elizabeth declared enthusiastically. "But the quickest way to work effectively for them is through woman's enfranchisement!"

When they parted, Elizabeth felt that she had found a true friend. If she could convince Susan to put woman's rights before every other cause, there was no telling what they might accomplish together!

14

DRINK AND DIVORCE

One bitterly cold evening in the early spring of 1852, Elizabeth sat at her desk in the cosy sitting room of her Seneca Falls home. A fire burned on the hearth, and at her elbow an oil lamp beamed softly. With the children and servants in bed and Henry away on a business trip, the house was very quiet. She took a deep breath, savoring the silence and solitude. Now she could set down on paper the phrases that had been forming in her mind as she rushed from crib to kitchen to preserve closet.

The older the boys grew, the more mischief they seemed to get into. Neil was nearly ten, Henry's namesake Kit was eight, Gat six, and their new little brother almost one year old. Elizabeth's sharp disappointment that he had not been a girl had soon dulled. She had not named this child after anyone but had given him a significant name of her own choosing, Theodore, which in her beloved Greek meant gift of god.

The three older boys were forever dreaming up games to play with little Ted. A few weeks ago they had harnessed themselves to his sled, and raced about the yard like fiery steeds. She had run out just in time to stop the sled and its precious cargo from careening over the edge of the bluff.

It was wonderful to have four healthy sons, but it was also very strenuous! At times she thought she would give almost anything for a few minutes of peace and quiet. Well now she must make good use of her opportunity to write, and get to work on her speech for the first Woman's State Temperance Convention to be held on April 20 in Rochester. Susan B. Anthony had asked her to preside.

Temperance was a cause dear to Elizabeth's heart. Had she not seen the degrading influence of drink all around her from her childhood days? As a young girl she had learned to avoid passing near bars and taverns, from which men were wont to stumble, sometimes groggy, often violent. She had seen women in her father's office who had suffered from the cruelty of drunken husbands.

Women had taken a great step forward in forming societies for temperance, but Elizabeth doubted that they could make permanent headway until they should gain the ballot. She would like to tell the women assembled in Rochester that they could best achieve their purpose by working for woman's enfranchisement, but she knew that Susan would not approve. Someday Susan must see the logic of Elizabeth's view. Meanwhile Elizabeth would put her best effort into the convention, as she had into the Seneca Falls gathering.

That first Woman's Rights Convention had been the spark that touched off a conflagration. On all sides women were rising to denounce evil and to demand reforms. Convention followed convention all over the country. What a long way women had come in four years, and over what a rocky road.

As Elizabeth dipped her pen into her silver-topped inkwell, her eye lit upon a neatly folded sheet of paper covered with firmly formed characters. Why had she set aside this letter for even one day?

It was from Susan B. Anthony. Dear Susan! How their

friendship had grown in the months since they had met. Letters had flown back and forth, and Susan had made frequent visits to the Stanton home. At her request the boys had begun to call her Aunt Susan. And she had asked Elizabeth and Henry to call her Susan, although she continued to address them as Mr. and Mrs. Stanton. Probably out of deference to our seniority, Elizabeth thought, although I am only five years older.

While Elizabeth was busy with her home and babies, Susan was out around the countryside ringing doorbells and speaking to women's societies to raise money for the cause of temperance. Now she was asking Elizabeth for practical advice in composing and delivering speeches, for which she had neither aptitude nor liking, she claimed.

Speaking in public was not so bad once one began, Elizabeth reflected. It was like taking a cold bath, the latest health fad. One found it horribly difficult to take the plunge, and the shock at first was paralyzing, but having experienced and survived the ordeal, one was eager to try it again.

All Susan needed was confidence, Elizabeth decided. If she could just forget herself, she would be a moving and effective speaker. There were practical steps to take, too. She would share what she had learned from her experience.

My dear Susan, Elizabeth wrote. *I have no doubt that a little practice will render you an admirable lecturer. But you must dress loosely, take a great deal of exercise, be particular about your diet, and sleep enough. . . . If you are attacked in your meetings, be good-natured and keep cool, and if you are simple and truth-loving, no sophistry can confound you.*

Now she must marshal her thoughts for her own address

to the convention. She wanted to make her speech as stirring as possible. But how should she go about it?

Elizabeth had just spread out a fresh sheet of paper when there came a pounding on the front door. Who could it be at this late hour? A fugitive slave would not be so bold, but would tap furtively at the back door, or on the window. Taking the lamp in her hand, she went into the hallway and opened the door. Shivering on the doorstep were a terrified small girl and boy.

"Please, ma'am, won't ye come? The ould man is poundin' Ma and is like to kill her."

Elizabeth recognized the two as part of the horde of immigrant offspring inhabiting rough huts down by the canal. To these children and their friends she had given fruit from her trees in the summer, and warm clothing and books in the winter. Shrugging into her coat, she ran down the hill with them.

The cottage they led her to was squalid, its small windows faintly lit. Inside a few dying coals on the hearth made a feeble glow. Elizabeth could barely distinguish two figures in a corner, whence issued agonized groans. A heavyset fellow bent over a crouched woman, striking her repeatedly with his fists.

How could a man be so brutish? Elizabeth's fury crowded out any fear for her own safety. Swiftly she marched to the man's side, seized him by the collar, jerked him to a chair, and pushed him into it.

Standing over him, stretching up as far as possible, she ordered fiercely, "Stay there, and behave yourself!" Unconsciously she used the same words with which she addressed her sons when they exasperated her beyond reason. Some of her deep anger must have penetrated the man's alcoholic fog. He stared at her, but sat quietly.

Elizabeth went to the woman and helped her to her feet. Even in the dim light she could see her bruised and battered face. But a moment later she realized that her suffering was due to more than the beating. She was also in deep labor.

Whether the husband's mistreatment had brought on the situation, Elizabeth did not know. But she must have help.

"Go and fetch Granny Sullivan," she told the children. "Tell her to come as fast as she can."

Then she led the mother to the one bedstead and covered her with a ragged blanket. The house was frigid. They must have light and heat. Ah, there was the stump of a candle on the table. Elizabeth lit it from the hearth, then went outside and found a wet coal pile, dug out some coal from its center and fed the fire. It sputtered, but revived.

The woman's groans were becoming more insistent. Where was the midwife? She should be here by now. Elizabeth went to the bedside. A few minutes later the woman cried out in anguish, and gave birth to a scrawny infant.

Frantically Elizabeth looked around the wretched shack. She needed something for tying the umbilical cord, an instrument to cut it with, and clean cloths. Aside from a few soiled garments hanging on nails in the wall, there appeared to be nothing available.

Then footsteps sounded. A stout woman entered, bearing a heavy basket. "I told the kids to get into my bed," she panted. "It was nice and warm, and they were like two bits of ice, poor things."

The midwife's wispy hair straggled out from under a man's battered hat, and her smile was toothless, but Elizabeth had never been more relieved to see anyone as she was this woman and the contents of her basket, which contained materials necessary to the occasion.

Together they worked over the woman and child. In a few minutes the baby gave a weak cry. The midwife examined it dourly. "Another he," she said, "to put some poor girl in trouble."

During all the proceedings the husband sat in his chair, slumped in a drunken stupor.

An hour later, as Elizabeth made ready to leave, the mother said weakly, "I'll never be able to thank ye rightly, ma'am. If ye hadn't come when ye did, both me and the babe would be dead." She shot a glance laden with hatred and contempt at the insensible man.

Heavy hearted, Elizabeth climbed the hill to her home. The fire was almost out, the lamp burning low. But there was no sleep in her. Her own comfort could wait. Women like the poor creature she had just left could not.

Picking up her pen, she wrote at the top of the sheet: *Divorce*. She would include a demand for it in her remarks to the first Woman's State Temperance Convention. She would tell them that women should divorce confirmed drunkards. Her pen flew over the paper.

In Rochester, three weeks later, dressed in a new short dress of rich black satin with matching trousers, Elizabeth surveyed with pride the five hundred women assembled. Was it only four years ago that she and her Quaker friends were considered outrageously daring to call a women's meeting in Seneca Falls? Today such gatherings were accepted as a matter of course.

"How my heart throbs," she said at the beginning of her speech, "to see women assembling together in convention, to inquire what part they have to take in the great moral struggles of humanity."

She went on to describe the suffering caused women by their drunken husbands. She urged them to cut down on the vast amounts of liquor sold by not using alcohol in their homes in any form, not even in cooking. They could spread the message of temperance also by lectures, tracts, and organizations.

Then, recalling anew the agony of the woman in childbirth whom she had rescued from her husband, Elizabeth lifted her head high and spoke out with all her force the words she had written late that fateful winter's night.

"Let no wife remain in the relation of wife with a confirmed drunkard. Let no drunkard be the father of thy children."

As the full meaning of her words reached the audience, many women put their fingers to their lips in shocked dismay. Was Mrs. Stanton recommending *aloud* and *in public* that women seek *divorce?* When no one in polite society so much as mentioned the word except in a whisper?

As Elizabeth continued, she could see women exchanging horrified glances. She could hear comments, such as, "No *decent* woman would want a divorce. It would be too much of a disgrace."

The sooner people got over the feeling that the dissolving of marriage bonds was tantamount to a pact with the devil, the sooner women, and men too, could be freed from unsuitable and degrading unions. A good marriage, like hers and Henry's, was beautiful beyond belief. A bad marriage must be unspeakably frightful. She continued courageously.

"Let us petition our State government so to modify the laws affecting marriage and the custody of children that a drunkard shall have no claims on either wife or child."

When she sat down, the hall was buzzing with outraged comments. To her amazement the gathering elected her president of the newly formed Woman's State Temperance Society.

Obviously some women could set aside their sense of delicacy and see the need for reform even in the so-called holy institution of marriage. All they needed was someone to speak out freely and frankly against intolerable situations. If this was to be her contribution to humanity's needs, she would keep on. Heaven knew there were situations enough that needed changing—especially the control of government. Just wait until women had a voice in that!

15

AT THE CAPITOL

*O*ne sleety morning in December of 1853, Elizabeth stood by the big, black kitchen range, stirring a large pan of custard, and keeping one eye on her long-awaited, precious baby daughter, Margaret, now a rosy toddler who moved uncertainly from chair to cupboard to table. A fearless climber, she would pull herself up to the top of the cupboard unless restrained. She had even been found once on the piano and another time on the bookcase.

Elizabeth looked out the window at the slashing storm. She hoped that Amelia Willard, her beloved, capable housekeeper, would be able to return soon from her aunt's funeral. From the front of the house came the sound of racing feet as the four boys chased from room to room. She must tell them to be quiet so that they would not disturb the two maids, both ill of stomach disorders.

If only she could prepare enough food and make the house presentable before her guests arrived on the afternoon train!

Suddenly the kitchen door burst open, and young Gerrit shot into the room, knocking the baby over in his haste.

"This just came," he announced breathlessly, as he handed his mother a letter.

"Can't you look where you're going?" Elizabeth scolded. She stooped and picked up the screeching Maggie, stroking the soft little arms, savoring the fragrance of her baby curls.

When Maggie had quieted, Elizabeth sat down at the table, the child on her lap, and opened the letter. It was from her dear Susan B. Anthony.

Elizabeth's eyes ran over the words. Susan was in charge of arrangements for the New York State Woman's Rights Convention to be held in February.

For a moment Elizabeth's thoughts ran back to a little more than a year ago, when Susan had attended her first woman's rights convention in Syracuse. She had met and talked with Ernestine Rose, the courageous Jewish lecturer; Dr. Harriot K. Hunt of Boston, one of the first women physicians; Lucy Stone, an antislavery lecturer and defender of equal educational opportunities for women; Antoinette Brown, the first woman to be ordained as a minister; Lucretia and James Mott, and Lucretia's sister, Martha C. Wright; and Gerrit Smith and his daughter.

Already alerted by Elizabeth to the need for reform in woman's status, Susan had been fully convinced at the meeting that only through enfranchisement could woman gain her rightful place. She had been elected secretary of the Syracuse convention, and from that time on had plunged into the work for women's rights with zeal and indefatigable energy.

Elizabeth read on, jogging Maggie on her knee. The high point of the state convention was to be an address before the joint judiciary committees of the legislature on the legal disabilities of women. There was only one woman who could do the subject justice, Susan wrote. That woman was Elizabeth Cady Stanton!

For a moment Elizabeth sat in stunned astonishment. Then, elated, she jumped up. With Maggie in her arms, she danced gaily around the kitchen, while the baby crowed in delight.

"What do you think of your mother being asked to address the legislature?" Elizabeth asked the happy infant. "Do you know what an honor that is for our sex?"

Suddenly, in the midst of a whirl, she stopped stock-still. To be invited to speak was an honor, certainly. It was also a terrifying responsibility.

On the stove the forgotten custard boiled up and out onto the hot metal surface. The acrid odor of burned milk and eggs filled the room. Elizabeth set Maggie down on the floor, and pulled the pot off the fire. She had so much work to do just keeping her brood fed and clothed and tended. How could she possibly take on so weighty and awesome a task? Where would she find the time to write and deliver so important a speech?

Then for a moment the years slipped away. Once more she was a small girl sitting in her father's office, and he was saying, "When you are grown up and able to prepare a speech, you could go to Albany and talk to the members of the legislature. You could tell them about the women who come into this office and the laws that are unfair to them. If you should convince the legislators to pass new laws, the old ones would no longer be in force."

Elizabeth threw back her shoulders. This invitation was her opportunity. This was the moment she had been working toward for many years. That its timing was not convenient to her was of no consequence. Somehow she would manage.

Picking the baby up in her arms, she marched out of the

kitchen, shutting the door firmly on the piles of dirty dishes, and the curdled custard in its pot. She sat down at her desk, and began to write:

DEAR SUSAN—

Can you get any acute lawyer . . . sufficiently interested in our movement to look up just eight laws concerning us—the very worst in all the code? I can generalize and philosophize easily enough of myself; but the details of the particular laws I need, I have not time to look up. You see, while I am about the house, surrounded by my children, washing dishes, baking, sewing, etc., I can think up many points, but I cannot search books, for my hands as well as my brains would be necessary for that work. . . .

To the baby at her feet, playing with the fire tongs, she said, "Oh, these lucky men. When they wish to write a document, they shut themselves up for days with their thoughts and their books. They have no idea of the difficulties a woman must surmount to get off a tolerable production!"

For weeks Elizabeth worked on her speech, her active mind searching out ideas while she managed her home and family, her pen racing over the page at night when she set her thoughts on paper.

She made plans to leave the five children in charge of Amelia and the maids. Then, a month before the convention, one of the boys by accident shot an arrow in the baby's eye. Mercifully, the missle struck in a corner of the eye, and no permanent damage was done, but Elizabeth was so alarmed she almost cancelled her plans to go to Albany. She would not have a moment's peace if she left all the children in Seneca Falls. The only way she could possibly go was to take the two youngest with her.

When, at last, she set out, she was accompanied by baby Margaret, three-year-old Theodore, and two nurses—one for each child.

At Johnstown she stopped for a short visit at her parents' home. How good it was to be welcomed by her mother, serene as always, and to feel her father's cool lips upon her cheek. In the old, familiar surroundings, where every piece of furniture had its special memories, Elizabeth could almost forget that she was the mother of five. It was easy to slip back into the role of daughter.

It was strange, she thought, how here in her childhood home she felt at once cherished—and threatened, as if within these walls she might lose all her hard-won independence. Of one thing she was certain. She would never place upon the little daughter asleep upstairs in the ancestral cradle any of the ridiculous restrictions under which she herself had suffered.

At family prayers, all of Elizabeth's youthful rebellion returned when Judge Cady chose to read from the Bible the fourteenth chapter of I Corinthians in which Paul adjured: *Let your women keep silence in the churches; for it is not permitted unto them to speak . . . it is a shame for women to speak in church.*

Later her father invited her into his law office. She went with him apprehensively, swept by the old uncertainties of her youth, when his opinions had all the strength of established law, and her own ideas seemed weak and untried. The judge was over eighty now, and with his finely molded head appeared more than ever the embodiment of wisdom.

On his desk was a copy of the *Albany Evening Journal*. To her alarm and delight she could see an announcement of the speech to be given by Elizabeth Cady Stanton, daughter of the distinguished jurist, Daniel Cady. He held it out to her, the tremor of his heavily veined hand betraying his agitation.

"I presume you can understand how disturbed I am that my daughter, reared in an atmosphere of refinement and dignity, should so forget her upbringing as to coarsen herself in this way like a *common* person," he said in a shaking voice. "Elizabeth, do you realize that no *lady* has ever before addressed the legislature?"

In as calm a tone as she could muster, Elizabeth replied, "Yes, Father, and I am proud to be the first *woman* to be chosen for that honor."

"Honor—harrumph!" the judge exclaimed. "If you should decline this, er, recognition, I would make it worth your while. I have heard you say that you would like to have the deed to the Seneca Falls house."

It was true. Ever since the passage of the married woman's property act in 1848 she had wanted to have legal title to her home. Father must be more deeply disturbed than she had realized to stoop to bribery. She must not let him know how sorely tempted she was. She must not give in.

"I am sorry, but all arrangements have been made," she said, miserable at the thought of hurting him and losing the chance of owning her home.

He cleared his throat, and placed the tips of his fingers together in the old familiar gesture. "Well, then, since my name seems to be involved with yours in this folly, suppose you read me what you intend to say."

Falteringly she began. How difficult it was to voice to this parent opinions about which she could speak easily to others. But as she proceeded, some of her usual confidence returned. By the time she had concluded, she felt that it was indeed a good speech. She looked up to see tears in her father's eyes. Ah, she thought, I've succeeded in awakening his sympathy for women who suffer under unjust laws.

But when he spoke, she was shocked by his reaction.

"Surely, Elizabeth, you have had a happy, comfortable life, with all your wants and needs supplied, and yet that speech fills me with self-reproach," he said, his voice deep with emotion. "How can a young woman, tenderly brought up, who has had no bitter personal experience, feel so keenly the wrongs of her sex? Where did you learn this lesson?"

"I learned it here in your office when a child," she said. "Don't you remember how I used to sit over there in the corner and listen to their complaints? I used to get so distressed over their sorrow! Surely you remember the night you explained how laws were made, and you told me that if I wanted to help women like your clients I should go to the legislature and make a speech in favor of new and better laws."

"*I* said *that?*" Daniel Cady asked in astonishment.

"Yes, Father. I am only doing what you suggested long ago. You said if I were a man I could introduce reform bills, but as a woman I could have no part in lawmaking. Then you told me I could try to persuade the men in office to change the laws. That is what I hope to do."

"So?" Her father had never looked at her more piercingly, "Well, then, let me make a suggestion."

Elizabeth's heart sank. Was he going to ask her to delete some parts? But he continued, "You have made your points clear and strong, but I think I can find you even more cruel laws than you have quoted."

Astounded, Elizabeth sat speechless while he cited the passages and made the necessary changes in her manuscript. At one o'clock in the morning they kissed each other good night. Elizabeth thought she had never felt so close to her father, not even in her childhood days. It seemed as if her refusal to bend to his will had been a bridge to understanding.

A few days later, when she stood on the platform of the Senate Chamber, she again knew panic. At least she did not have to fear ridicule for her dress. She had forsaken the bloomer costume except for home use, and wore today a long gown of rich black silk with white lace at her throat and wrists. For all her thirty-eight years, she felt as nervous as long ago when, the only girl in the Greek class, she was called upon to translate a difficult passage. Then she calmed. Today she would translate to the men here assembled the difficult and unfair position of women.

"We have every qualification required by the Constitution necessary to the legal voter, but the one of sex," she said, making her voice low and clear. "We are moral, virtuous, intelligent, and in all respects quite equal to the proud white man himself, and yet by your laws we are classed with idiots, lunatics, and Negroes. . . .

"Now, gentlemen, we would fain know by what authority you have disfranchised one-half the people of this State? You who have so boldly taken possession of the bulwarks of this republic, show us your credentials; and thus prove your exclusive right to govern, not only yourselves, but us."

Elizabeth then cited examples of woman's unjust legal sta-

tus as wife, mother, and widow: "The wife who inherits no
property holds about the same legal position that does the
slave on the Southern plantation. She can own nothing and
sell nothing. She has no right even to the wages she earns;
her person, her time, her services are the property of another. She cannot testify in many cases against her husband.
She can get no redress for wrongs in her own name in any
court of justice. She can neither sue nor be sued. She is not
held responsible for any crime committed in the presence of
her husband. . . .

"A husband has the right to whip his wife, to shut her up
in a room, and administer whatever chastisement he may
deem necessary to insure obedience to his wishes. . . .

"He can forbid all persons harboring or trusting her on
his account. He can deprive her of all social intercourse with
her nearest and dearest friends.

"If by great economy she accumulates a small sum, which
for future need she deposits little by little in a savings bank,
the husband has a right to draw it out at his option, to use as
he may see fit."

Telling of one grievance after another, Elizabeth forgot
her own fears. She recited instances of fathers apprenticing
their sons to gamblers and saloon-keepers, and binding their
daughters out to owners of brothels, and of men on their
deathbeds willing the guardianship of their children away
from their wives.

A woman separated from her husband, she said, no matter
how despicable a character he might be, had no jurisdiction
over the children, but must surrender them to his doubtful
care. A widow whose husband had died without making a
will received only one third of his estate.

"Would to God you could know the burning indignation that fills woman's soul when she turns over the pages of your statute books," Elizabeth cried, "and sees there how like feudal barons you free men hold your women. Would you could know the humiliation she feels for her sex when she thinks of . . . the lordly, absolute rights of man over all women, children, and property."

Never before in her experience as a speaker had Elizabeth been accorded such rapt attention. She could feel every eye upon her as she finished, "Let us say, in behalf of the women of this State, we ask for all that you have asked for yourselves in the progress of your development since the *Mayflower* cast anchor beside Plymouth Rock; and simply on the ground that the rights of every human being are the same and identical."

The thunder of applause was like the sweetest music. Was it proof that she had won over these men? Trembling, Elizabeth sat down.

Alas for her hopes! The legislators refused to change the laws regarding woman's status.

Time sped by so rapidly that Elizabeth often felt as if she were caught in a fast current, being propelled along too swiftly to enjoy the voyage or view the scenery.

In January 1856 she gave birth to her sixth child. To her great joy the baby was another girl, and was promptly named Harriet Eaton after Elizabeth's beloved sister. Three years later Elizabeth delivered her seventh and last infant, a son, Robert.

With seven children to care and plan for, many women would have felt that they had enough to occupy all their time and energy. Not so Elizabeth. She continued her wide correspondence with individuals in the women's rights movement, she wrote extensive articles, and she took part in conventions when possible. If unable to attend, she wrote the announcement, the opening address, and the resolutions.

Her friendship with Susan B. Anthony broadened and deepened. Susan, tired and discouraged in her travels around the country to raise money and obtain signatures, often wrote to Elizabeth for help in composing speeches. And Elizabeth, in the midst of preserving cherries or mending children's clothes, made time for penning words that would help to free women. It was a joke between them that Elizabeth forged the thunderbolts and Susan delivered them, slowly overcoming her fear of the platform.

When Elizabeth was too beset by family duties to concentrate on her writings, Susan came to the Stanton house and capably looked after the children, even administering spankings upon occasion. Each woman gave to the other much-needed moral and spiritual support.

When little Bob was seven months old, Elizabeth was shocked by the news of John Brown's raid on Harper's Ferry, Virginia. Almost immediately she learned that her beloved cousin Gerrit Smith was suspected of being an accomplice.

Knowing Gerrit's hatred for all forms of violence, Elizabeth was certain that he might approve wholeheartedly of Brown's freeing slaves, but not of his seizure of the United States arsenal. Then came word from Libby that her father had suffered a nervous collapse.

There was sorrow, too, within the Cady family. Judge Cady, who for many years had overworked his one good eye, had awakened on a spring morning to a world of darkness. He accepted his blindness with an equanimity that to Elizabeth was heartbreaking. To see her once independent father being led from room to room was almost more than she could bear.

On October 30, 1859, Daniel Cady died. Elizabeth was tortured by regrets. Of all his children she had given him the most anxiety and concern. Why had she rebelled so openly against his views? Why had she not used more tact and patience? If only she had waited a bit, she might have avoided giving him pain. Poor man, he had been so distressed over her insistence upon speaking at Junius that he had disinherited her. And once he took a stand, he rarely reversed his decision. Elizabeth was certain that she would have no share in his estate.

Taking the baby with her, Elizabeth hurried to Johnstown to be with her mother and sisters for the funeral. When the Judge's will was read aloud to the assembled family, Elizabeth's name was included with the others. That Father had changed his mind on this one point was a comfort to her. Perhaps it was his way of telling her that he thought her demand for women's rights had merit, after all, just as his assistance in citing laws for her speech to the New York Legislature had indicated some sympathy for women's cause.

Back home in Seneca Falls, Elizabeth was restless and distraught. Writing to Susan she deplored her "dwarfed womanhood" and longed to do the work of a "full grown man" in the cause of freedom.

Then came a letter from Susan asking Elizabeth to speak again in Albany, this time on behalf of amendments to the woman's property law of 1848 at a joint session of the New York State Legislature.

Once more Elizabeth was beset by overwhelming domestic problems. But once more she determined to make the most of the opportunity to further woman's cause. Susan came for a visit and assisted with the care of the children, freeing Elizabeth for long hours of thought and concentration in a quiet room.

On March 19, 1860, Elizabeth spoke for the second time in the New York State Capitol. This time she stood at the speaker's desk, facing a joint session of the legislature and packed galleries, and demanded for woman the rights of a citizen.

"When you talk, gentlemen, of sheltering woman from the rough minds and revolting scenes of real life, you must be either talking for effect, or be wholly ignorant of what the facts of life are," she said. "The man, whatever he is, is known to the woman. She is the companion not only of the statesman, the orator, and the scholar—but the vile, vulgar, brutal man has his mother, his wife, his sister, his daughter . . . and if man shows out what he is anywhere, it is at his own hearthstone. . . . Gentlemen, such scenes as woman has witnessed at her own fireside, where no eye save Omnipotence could pity, no strong arm could help, can never be realized at the polls."

For over an hour Elizabeth spoke in her clear, compelling voice to a rapt audience. Later she listened to words of highest praise. No man in the entire country could surpass her eloquence, people said. That was all very flattering, she thought, but the real test would be the action of the lawmakers.

The next day the bill passed the legislature and was signed

by the governor! Elizabeth could hardly believe the good news.

The new law vastly enlarged the scope of woman's activities. Under it a married woman had the right to own property, both real and personal. She could collect her wages and invest them without her husband's interference. She could now buy, sell, and make contracts with her husband's consent. If he were a convict, insane, a confirmed drunkard, or had deserted her, she could act without his consent. She could sue and be sued. She was the joint guardian with her husband of their children. And should her husband die, she would have the same rights as he would have at her death.

Now, thought Elizabeth, the Flora Campbells could not be driven out of their rightful homes, mothers would not have their children torn from their arms and sold to unscrupulous men, widows could inherit all their husbands' property.

Through Elizabeth's mind flashed a memory of that long-ago day when she was a small child and her father had outlined the steps by which she might improve the legal status of woman. If only he could know that she had indeed taken those steps and succeeded in bettering woman's condition to such an extent.

If only Father had lived a few months longer! How she wished she might say to him today, "Father, I have done what you said. Are you not convinced now that a daughter can be as effective as a son?"

16

WOMEN AND THE CIVIL WAR

*L*ate one summer afternoon in 1863 Elizabeth and Susan and four of the seven Stanton children sat at the big table in the dining room of their home in New York City, where they had moved in 1862 after Henry was appointed to a position in the Customs House office. It had been difficult to leave their home and friends in Seneca Falls, but since the launching of the women's rights movement fifteen years before and its tremendous growth throughout the country, Elizabeth felt that she could more effectively help to direct its activities from a central location. Besides, here in the city the three older boys, ranging in age from seventeen to twenty-one, could continue their education at college and law school without having to leave home.

Like women and children in homes all over the country, the Stantons and Susan were scraping lint. Elizabeth and Maggie cut old linen into small squares which the others unraveled. In the middle of the table was a soft pile of fluffy white fibers, to which each person added from time to time. The lint would be used for soldiers' surgical dressings. In this third year of the Civil War the casualties were catastrophic, and the need for medical supplies unending.

Twelve-year-old Theodore lifted his eyes from his work. "Jim Brown says that I'm a sissy to do this, and that only stupid girls and women should spend their time this way."

"What's that?" Elizabeth demanded sharply.

"I was only telling you what Jim said," Theodore remarked with a grin.

"And Jim, I dare say, was only repeating what he had heard from his father or some other misguided male," Elizabeth rasped.

"Women are not half as stupid as the men who started the war!" Harriot declared heatedly.

Elizabeth heard her with satisfaction. At seven Harriot was a spirited defender of her sex. She was also of an independent mind, and now spelled her name with an *O* instead of the customary *E*, as did the aunt for whom she had been named.

Little Robert, the youngest, sighted along an imaginary rifle. In his soft four-year-old voice he declared, "Bang, bang! I want to be a soldier."

"I pray that you may never be one," Susan declared vehemently, true to her Quaker principles. "War is wicked, and don't you forget it."

"Papa says war is necessary if we are to free the slaves," Maggie said. At ten she was apt to quote her parents as if they were oracles, sometimes to their discomfiture.

"What do you think the Emancipation Proclamation did?" Theodore asked in a superior tone. "It made the slaves 'henceforth and forever free.' "

"What did Papa mean, then?" Maggie asked.

"That only by winning the war and passing new laws for the entire country can we be sure that slavery will really be abolished," Elizabeth said. "That is why we formed the Woman's National Loyal League. It gives women a high purpose to think about while they are knitting socks, preserving food, and gathering supplies for the soldiers."

"And scraping lint!" Harriot added.

In May Elizabeth and Susan had launched the League, which was devoted to influencing public opinion to demand that this be a war for freedom. An office had been established with Susan in charge of obtaining signatures to petitions demanding that Congress pass an amendment abolishing slavery. After working there all day, she was helping with the lint until dinnertime.

Now Susan looked up from her linen scraping. "I cannot help but feel that we have made a terrible mistake to set aside our work for woman's rights because of the war."

Was Susan right? Elizabeth wondered. Women's organizations had been making great headway just before the outbreak of hostilities. State and local groups were forging ahead, with officers who were seasoned workers of ten to fifteen years in the field. There was hardly a town that did not have a band of women working for enfranchisement.

Elizabeth had labored indefatigably. In addition to carrying on an extensive correspondence with women and men who believed in equal rights, she had written countless articles and attended more conventions than she could remember, usually conducting the meeting and giving the chief address.

Much of the credit for the movement's growth was due to Susan's tireless and methodical work. She had traveled in all kinds of weather, even to remote villages, to open women's eyes to the need for elevating their status and to raise money. She wrote innumerable letters and encouraged thousands of workers. But when war was declared, patriotic fervor had crowded out all other causes.

"Don't worry," Elizabeth said cheerfully. "We women

must do all we can now to save the Union and free the slaves. After the war is won, the men will see how valuable we were, and they'll reward us with the ballot."

"I wish I had your optimism," Susan said dourly. "I am afraid it won't be as simple as that."

"You wait and see," Elizabeth said with more confidence than she felt. "Remember our resolution—that there can never be a true peace in this Republic until the civil and po-litical rights of all citizens of African descent and *all women* are practically established. The men at the League meeting voted in approval of that."

"A good many people objected, too," Susan said. "They accused you of dragging in woman's rights."

Suddenly through the open window came an ominous roar.

"What's that?" Harriot demanded.

The group hurried to the parlor in the front of the house and looked out. Neil ran down the stairs and joined them. A tall, well-built, handsome man of twenty-one, he had been studying in his bedroom. "It must be the fellows that are op-posing the draft," he said. "I had heard there might be riots, but I didn't think they'd come this far uptown."

Elizabeth, too, had heard of riot threats. The newly passed draft law to fill the fast-emptying ranks of the Union Army had aroused terrific opposition, especially among the poorer classes, who objected violently to the fact that any man who could pay three hundred dollars for a substitute would be exempted from service. Who could afford as much as three hundred dollars? shouted the dock hands, ditch dig-gers, clerks and stockboys, rage overruling reason.

With a complete lack of logic they blamed the war on the

Negroes, arguing that the draft was all the fault of the Negroes and their champions, those high-falutin' folks the abolitionists. It was time to show the black men a lesson, and their antislavery friends, as well. Lynch a few of them, burn their houses. See if they wouldn't sing a different tune.

All this passed through Elizabeth's mind as she peered down the street. In the distance she could make out a seething mass of men, waving weapons, and approaching with frightening speed. As abolitionists, she and Henry—Susan too—would be in danger.

The children! They must not be victims of mob violence! Where would they be safe? Her mind raced in anguish. Ah, the roof! They could remain there undetected. And if the house were set afire, they could escape over the rooftops. Hastily she herded the four before her, calling to the servants to follow. She hurried them all up to the attic and opened the skylight, placing a large chest beneath it. Then she descended to the front hall where Susan waited. By now the mob was only half a block distant.

"Where is Neil?" Elizabeth asked.

"Out there," Susan said, pointing to the front steps.

Elizabeth opened the door. "Neil, come in at once."

"Oh, Mother," he said, "you're getting upset over nothing. I want to see what's going on."

Now the rioters were abreast of the house. "Ain't that one of them abolitionists now?" a man shouted, pointing at Elizabeth.

"Get back inside, Mother, and lock the door," Neil said, giving her a shove.

"Neil!" she implored, but in vain.

Jauntily he descended the stairs to the street and greeted

the oncoming mob. "You don't think that my mother's one of *those?*" he demanded with a grin.

"Lookit him! He's one of those three-hundred-dollar guys!" jeered a red-faced man. "Let's teach him a thing or two."

Before Elizabeth and Susan's horrified eyes, Neil was taken roughly by the arms and hurried away, a part of the jostling, shouting mob.

Elizabeth's heart was pounding. What would happen to her firstborn, her precious son? Fear such as she had never known flooded her.

Susan, too, was white-faced. But she was calm. "Now remember, Mrs. Stanton, that Neil is of age and able to take care of himself. You must not be afraid for him any more than you were for yourself when the mayor of Albany had to escort us from our hotel to the hall."

How well Elizabeth remembered the evening when she and Susan, with Lucretia Mott, Martha C. Wright, Gerrit Smith, and Frederick Douglass were scheduled to speak against slavery. They had been on tour in New York State, and had been threatened and harassed on every occasion. So dangerous were the mobs in Albany that Mayor Thatcher himself had escorted the speakers to the hall, thrown a cordon of police around it, and sat on the platform with a loaded revolver ready to quell any attempt at disturbance.

Now Elizabeth wondered if the maddened men in the street would recognize her house as the home of antislavery workers. If so, they would surely storm it. Trembling, she tried to decide what to do in such an event. Phrases began forming in her mind.

"If those men break down the door," she told Susan, "I

shall speak to them as Americans and citizens of a republic and appeal to their reason."

"It will take more than reason to stop those creatures!" Susan warned.

As the women watched, the mob surged onward. One man uprooted a paling from a fence across the way and swung it over his head. Another picked up a flowerpot and flung it against the door. Its thud echoed through the hall, but no footsteps followed it.

One minute the street was full of men. The next, there were only the backs of those in the rear, straggling down the road.

Trembling, Elizabeth gave a deep sigh. Her younger children and home were safe. But there was still Neil! She was consumed with anxiety.

An hour later there was a knock on the back door. Elizabeth ran to unlock it, and saw Neil's face.

"Oh, Neil!" she cried, and flung the door wide. "Whatever happened?"

"Nothing much," he said airily. "We went past a saloon, so I invited some of the fellows in for a drink. It was a good thing I had some money with me. They asked me to join them in a toast to Jeff Davis."

"And what did you do?" Elizabeth asked.

He gave a sheepish grin. "I'm not as brave as you are, Mother. There were two dozen of them, and only one of me. I drank to him."

"And then?" Elizabeth asked.

"While they were giving three cheers for Old Jeff, I slipped out through a side door. And here I am."

When Henry came home later that evening, accompanied

by Kit and Gat, who had gone to his office for safety, he reported that in other parts of the city Negroes had been shot and hung on lamp posts, and abolitionists' homes burned. They would all spend the night with Tryphena and Edward Bayard, he said, and the next day Elizabeth must go with the children to Johnstown.

On her return to the city, Elizabeth learned that there had been more than a thousand casualties, and that over one million dollars' worth of property had been destroyed. Susan had attempted to remain in the city, pursuing her work for the Loyal League, but had been forced to go to relatives on Staten Island, where she waited until order was restored by the army.

By August of the following year, the Woman's Loyal League had amassed 400,000 signatures on petitions to free all slaves. And in 1865 the Thirteenth Amendment, abolishing slavery, was passed on the recommendation of President Lincoln.

Elizabeth felt the pride of satisfaction. Now the country could get on with the work of universal suffrage, securing the franchise for Negroes and women. For a time all the nation was deep in sorrow over the death of Lincoln. Later Elizabeth plunged into the new effort, presiding at the initial meeting of the American Equal Rights Association in New York, which combined the efforts of the antislavery and woman's rights movements.

A few months later Elizabeth received in the mail an envelope containing copies of bills proposed to enfranchise the Negro. She was reading one of them when she stopped in horrified amazement. Surely she could not be seeing correctly. She peered at the paper.

There was no doubt about it. The word *male* was written into the amendment, giving men the exclusive right to vote! Its presence meant the exclusion of all females from the privileges and responsibilities of voting.

Immediately Elizabeth and Susan alerted other women workers. They began to protest. Why, they demanded, should the enfranchisement of Negro men be any more important than the enfranchisement of all women?

From one after another of the men who had formerly been in favor of woman suffrage came declarations that the two causes should not be confused. And from many women came word that they should not obstruct the Negro's cause, but should step aside and await their turn. This was the Negro's hour!

Even Wendell Phillips, who had spoken out boldly in behalf of admitting women delegates to the 1840 World Anti-Slavery Convention in London, and who had advocated the enfranchisement of women for many years, often appearing on the same platform with Elizabeth and Susan—even he, whom they regarded as the most staunch of allies and friends, turned a deaf ear to pleas. No, he would not endanger the passage of the bill to enfranchise Negroes by including women.

It was wrong to mix the cause of woman with that of the Negro, Phillips wrote to Elizabeth. *I think such a mixture would lose for the Negro far more than we should gain for the woman.*

Infuriated, Elizabeth swiftly wrote back: *May I ask in reply to your fallacious letter just one question based on the apparent opposition in which you place the Negro and woman. My question is this: Do you believe the African race is composed entirely of males?*

Let Wendell Phillips answer that, she thought, as she marched furiously to the mail box.

In the great wave of activity to enfranchise the Negro, the women who had unselfishly set aside their own needs to help win the war were now brusquely pushed out of the way. Statesmen and politicians conveniently forgot women's work in the war—the gathering of signatures for the Thirteenth Amendment, the formation of the Sanitary Commission, the women nurses, the Freedman's Bureau for the relief of Negroes, and the efforts of countless individuals who had kept farms and businesses active so that husbands, fathers, and brothers might carry arms in the Union's defense.

What kind of reward was this for women who had labored to free the Negro?

Bitterly Elizabeth acknowledged that Susan had been indeed right. It had been a tragic mistake to interrupt their work for women's rights. Now they must begin again.

Indignantly Elizabeth and Susan circulated petitions to women in all parts of the country, the first ever to be addressed to the United States Congress on behalf of women's rights.

To the Senate and House of Representatives: The undersigned women of the United States respectfully ask an amendment to the Constitution that shall prohibit the several states from disfranchising any of their citizens on the ground of sex. Then followed several sound arguments in favor of suffrage for women.

Petitions with ten thousand signatures were presented to Congress in the 1865–1866 session.

With satisfaction Elizabeth and Susan read a speech by Senator Cowan of Pennsylvania to his colleagues about the leaders of the women's rights movement. "They have their banner flung out to the winds," he said. "Their cry is for justice, and you cannot deny it."

Elizabeth and Susan and other steadfast women, including Lucretia Mott, Martha C. Wright, and Ernestine Rose, worked frantically, writing articles for the press, addressing public gatherings, sending letters to influential people and legislators. But their almost superhuman effort was in vain against overwhelming opposition.

In spite of all their efforts, one state after another ratified the Fourteenth Amendment to the Constitution, limiting the franchise to male citizens.

To Elizabeth the news came as a bitter shock. How readily the men supporters of woman suffrage had forgotten their promises! How cruelly they had turned their backs on the women who had helped them with loyalty and devotion!

The war and its aftermath had taught her a bitter lesson, Elizabeth realized. Men could not be depended upon to aid women in their struggle for enfranchisement. From now on, Elizabeth decided, she would listen to Susan, and stand by her. Women must stand on their own feet, and devote every ounce of energy to their own cause. Never again would they step aside for others.

17

KANSAS

*G*ingerly Elizabeth stretched out on a folded carriage robe in the wagon bed, spreading her traveling cloak over her. Warm though the noonday sun had been, the autumn evening was cool here on the Kansas prairie. Above her head the sky was dotted with stars, the only light visible in all the broad expanse. The nearby cabin was a black blur in the surrounding shadows. From the grass came the sound of myriad insects.

Gradually Elizabeth began to relax. Perhaps tonight she would be able to sleep. With that hope she had decided to spend the night in the wagon, rather than the cabin, where the beds, as she had discovered in similar dwellings, were apt to be occupied by other than human beings. Of all the hardships of this speaking tour, the most difficult for her to bear were the bedbugs and body lice that abounded in many quarters where she was forced to stay, no hotels or inns being available in parts of this newly settled state.

There were other discomforts, too. The food was often almost inedible—bacon floating in its own grease, biscuits and bread green with soda, and coffee flavored with sorghum molasses.

Thank goodness for her strong body. It was an advantage on this trip to have a little excess flesh to depend upon, she thought wryly. Many days she felt as if she were like a camel, subsisting on its hump. The important thing was to keep her sense of humor, and not to let anything stand in the way of her mission here in the west.

What good news it had been in 1867 for Elizabeth and Susan and other women's rights workers to learn that in the recently admitted state of Kansas amendments to its constitution were being submitted to enfranchise women and Negroes!

The news was a ray of hope in a dark hour, and especially welcome after the failure of efforts to enfranchise women at the New York State Constitutional Convention that same year. Despite petitions galore, one with his own wife's name at its head, Horace Greeley, as chairman, had reported: "Your Committee does not recommend an extension of the elective franchise to women." So furious was he at Elizabeth's heated opposition, that he closed forever the columns of the *New York Tribune* to her.

When a plea had come from Kansas women for the most eloquent speakers in the movement to travel around the state arousing people to vote for women's rights, Susan had urged Elizabeth to accompany her on the tour.

How Elizabeth's spirits had soared! Beyond her wildest dreams had been the thought that one day she would go on a speaking tour of the West in the cause of woman suffrage. Then doubt assailed her. Was not her first duty to her family? Robert was only eight, and the girls eleven and fourteen. No, she had better stay at home.

Susan had persisted. Elizabeth would be a great attraction. Her name was well known across the country for her spirited demands for women. People would come from miles away to see her and to hear what she had to say for the cause of woman suffrage. As for the children, they could get along perfectly well under Amelia Willard's capable care.

Elizabeth pondered. Did she at this stage of her life have a right to follow her own desires and give a large portion of her time wholly to the work for women's rights? How tempting the prospect of spending two or three months in pursuance of a goal she deemed paramount! Yet, was she being selfish in wishing to be freed from family responsibilities for a little while in order to further the cause she loved?

Into her mind flashed Emma Willard's advice to her pupils. *It is questionable how far we have a right to sacrifice ourselves.* For years Elizabeth had stifled her desire to throw herself into the work for women's rights with the same complete dedication possible to Susan in her unmarried state.

That evening she had discussed the problem with Henry. At the prospect of her absence, his face had fallen. Then his brow had cleared. "If the tables were turned, and I were the one invited to speak on such a tour and for so worthy a cause, there would be no question of my accepting. You would be the first to make my way clear to go, just as you have made it possible for me to go off on countless business and speaking engagements all during our life together." He drew her to him tenderly. "God knows I'll miss you, but your place is in Kansas. If anyone can sway the voters, it is you, my dear."

At first the tour had not been unlike Elizabeth's trips around New York State. She and Susan had traveled by train to Kansas, and had spoken in large cities and towns. But Kansas was so big that there were many small settlements that could not be reached by train. Susan and Elizabeth had decided to separate and visit different areas, hoping to reach as many voters as possible. The former governor of Kansas, Charles Robinson, had offered to take Elizabeth in his carriage.

What an adventure the trip had been! Sometimes the roads were so dangerous that the governor had to lead the horses. When fording streams at night, he gave the reins to Elizabeth and walked ahead, taking off his coat so that she could see his white shirt in the darkness. Many times she had been rigid with terror lest the governor step into a deep hole and be drowned or the wagon overturn and she be thrown out and injured.

The thrill of working for the cause she loved had given her the strength and courage to continue. One night she spoke to a crowd gathered in an empty mill, the only light a single candle shining over her head. At other times she gave her talk in schoolhouses, churches, log cabins, depots, hotels, barns, and the open air.

Tomorrow they must drive many miles across unsettled plains to a new community of two dozen families. She must sleep so that she would be rested and alert. Pulling the cloak up around her shoulders, she began to drift off into slumber.

Suddenly a loud snorting and grunting aroused her, and the wagon began to shake. Fearfully Elizabeth looked down into the dim space beside the carriage. There were a number of long-nosed black pigs. The governor had warned her of their ferocity. The animals were jostling each other for a place at the iron steps of the carriage, against which each one vigorously scratched its back.

Good heavens! The pigs must be infested with fleas! The

scratching would dislodge them, and they would seek a new victim. If she were to avoid such an attack, she must keep the pigs away from the carriage.

Seizing a long leather whip from its socket, Elizabeth lashed it from side to side of the carriage. The pigs dispersed. But the moment she ceased her efforts, they renewed their scratching on the iron steps.

Alas for her hopes of a night's unbroken rest. Sleepily Elizabeth sat upright, dozing and nodding, but keeping the whip moving from side to side. The next night she was so fatigued that she kept to her verminous bed even when a mouse ran across her face.

Although Elizabeth and Susan put their whole hearts into the cause, they learned to their dismay that neither the Republican nor the Democratic party had come out in support of woman's enfranchisement. Then the St. Louis Woman Suffrage Association sent word to Susan that George Francis Train would speak in Kansas for two weeks endorsing woman suffrage!

Ebullient, generous, dramatic Mr. Train, a fabulously wealthy Democrat who aspired to the presidency, was scheduled to tour with one of the leading politicians of the state, who dropped out at the last minute. Susan took his place for the strenuous fortnight's campaign.

The energy and enthusiasm that Train had demonstrated in building clipper ships, selling American goods in Australia, traveling in China, India, and Russia, building England's first street railways, developing the far West, and initiating the Union Pacific Railway, he now applied to his campaign.

In a day when most men dressed in sober black and gray, Train wore a blue coat with brass buttons, a white vest, black trousers, patent leather boots, and lavender kid gloves. Tall and handsome, with a mass of curly brown hair, beard, and moustache, he capered and gestured his way about the platform, amusing his audience with his mimicry and pantomime.

What cheers there were from the audience when he shook his finger and shouted, "Every man in Kansas who throws a vote for the Negro and not for women has insulted his mother, his daughter, his sister, and his wife!"

During the campaign Susan grew to respect Train for his energy, even disposition, and cheerfulness under trying situations, although she disagreed strongly with his lack of sympathy for the Negro and his enmity for abolitionists in general, who attacked him fiercely. He retaliated by asking from the platform, "Where is Wendell Phillips today? Lost caste everywhere. Inconsistent in all things and cowardly in this. Where is Horace Greeley in this Kansas war for liberty? Pitching the woman suffrage idea out of the convention."

When Elizabeth and Susan met in Leavenworth for election day, they visited all the polling places in open carriages, and made speeches. The singing Hutchinsons were there, and sang:

> Who votes for woman suffrage now
> Will add new laurels to his brow;
> His children's children, with holy fire,
> Will chant in praise their patriot sire.
> No warrior's wreath of glory shed

A brighter lustre o'er the head
Than he who battles selfish pride,
And votes with woman side by side.

Elizabeth hardly heard their harmonious voices. She was too anxious about the results of the election and excited about some news Susan had just told her.

George Francis Train had offered to finance a weekly newspaper for the cause of woman suffrage!

A newspaper published for the sole purpose of promoting women's rights! Could it possibly be true? Elizabeth could hardly contain her elation. She and Susan had long wished for a regular and established outlet in which to conduct a continuous program of education and enlightenment toward the enfranchisement of women. Now that desire was to become a reality.

If only the offer had not come from so controversial a figure! Mr. Train had many enemies among abolitionists. Many old friends of the women's rights movement were bound to be alienated if its two foremost leaders were to ally themselves with him.

Elizabeth was hesitant about accepting the offer. But Susan was convinced that Mr. Train was essentially a high-minded, moral man, for all his dramatic posturing. He was the only one who had offered substantial help to the cause of woman suffrage. Heaven knew that women needed a champion at this juncture!

While Elizabeth hesitated, she recalled her difference of opinion with Susan at the time of the Civil War. Time had proved Susan to be right in fearing that men would desert woman's cause in favor of the Negro's.

What did it matter what other people thought? Susan's opinion meant more to Elizabeth than that of any other person in the movement. She pushed aside her doubts, and with Susan accepted the challenge.

To Elizabeth and Susan's deep disappointment, the voting men of Kansas refused enfranchisement to Negroes and to women. Elizabeth was not surprised; the forces working against the amendment were powerful and wealthy.

But although defeated in their aim, Elizabeth and Susan were not to creep home crestfallen. Instead they embarked with Mr. Train as his guests on a series of speaking engagements that had all the fanfare, if not the justification, of a triumphal tour.

Joining Train in Omaha, they spoke on woman suffrage to packed houses in St. Louis, Chicago, Springfield, Louisville, Cincinnati, Cleveland, Buffalo, Rochester, Syracuse, Albany, Springfield, Massachusetts, Worcester, Boston, and Hartford, ending with a flourish at Steinway Hall, New York, in mid-December.

18

THE REVOLUTION

*E*lizabeth could not help but note that passengers on the Philadelphia train sat up and took notice as she and her cousin Libby made their way into the parlor car in New York. She heard an elderly gentleman say in a piercing whisper, "The one with the bright blue eyes and pink cheeks is Elizabeth Cady Stanton. You must have heard her speak on women's rights. The other is Elizabeth Smith Miller, daughter of the philanthropist, Gerrit Smith."

As she set her capacious handbag on the floor beside her where she could keep an eye on its precious contents, Elizabeth said laughingly, "Now tell me just what Tryphena said to you."

Libby gave her a merry smile. "She hopes that you will settle down and stay at home like a respectable wife and mother now that you are editor of *The Revolution*."

Elizabeth laughed aloud. "What a ridiculous idea! Someday I shall ask her if she ever heard of a male editor worth his salt who sat at his desk all the time. She ought to know that news doesn't just walk into an editorial office."

"Tryphena wants you to be a model of propriety, just as she is," Libby said. "Do you remember how she actually wept real tears when we appeared in Johnstown long ago in our short skirts and trousers? And begged us not to wear them when we visited at her home?"

Elizabeth chuckled. "Tryphena is so proper that it hurts.

She considers me a disgrace to the family, especially now that I'm connected with a radical newspaper."

Despite her sister's disapproval, Elizabeth was thrilled to be working on *The Revolution*, with Susan as publisher, and Parker Pillsbury, an experienced journalist, reformer, and loyal friend of woman suffrage, sharing editorial responsibilities.

The Revolution, issued weekly, had as its slogan, "Down with politicians; up with the people." In its columns it supported principle not policy—"Educated suffrage irrespective of sex or color"—equal pay to women for equal work, eight-hour labor, and the abolition of standing armies and party despotisms.

Every issue carried witty, pithy, informative articles that Elizabeth penned on her favorite subjects, but over and above all, the cause of woman suffrage.

From the first *The Revolution* aroused antagonism among the conservatives of the woman's rights movement. The title alone was enough to shock many. But people needed to be shocked, Elizabeth and Susan felt. For far too long the unequal and degraded state of woman had been accepted with apathy and complacency.

How Elizabeth wished that Susan might have come on this trip to Philadelphia! But since Mr. Train had been obliged to withdraw his financial support, Susan had decided to remain in New York. She could not spare even one day from her work of soliciting support for the paper, she said. Subscriptions came in encouragingly, but they paid only a fraction of the newspaper's expenses. It was difficult enough to get advertisements for so controversial a publication.

What made her task more difficult was the fact that she and Elizabeth and Parker Pillsbury had decided not to accept advertising for quack medicines or anything they could not recommend in all sincerity. Day after day Susan trudged about the city in search of advertising for dependable products and selling subscriptions. It was discouraging, tiring work, but Susan with her indomitable spirit rarely seemed discouraged.

In the months since its launching, *The Revolution* had attacked every law and custom that kept woman in subjugation. Now Elizabeth and Susan were in the thick of an effort to improve the conditions of working women.

In many cases women were hired for less money than their male counterparts, prohibited from taking positions of management, held back from working overtime, and often forced to labor under conditions that were unhealthful, unsanitary, and downright dangerous. Over and over again, in editorials and news items, Elizabeth called attention to employment inequities.

Susan had organized a Working Woman's Association with a membership of typesetters, printers, bookbinders, factory workers, milliners, seamstresses, embroidery workers, and rag pickers. Through the organization Elizabeth and Susan attempted to improve working conditions, emphasizing always that the only effective way for women to better their lot was through the ballot. Until women should secure the right to vote, they would remain powerless to make legal progress.

At first loath to incur masculine disapproval and enmity, members of the Working Woman's Association were gradually seeing their need for a part in the lawmaking process. A widely publicized case of alleged infanticide had opened the eyes of many to their helplessness under the law.

Elizabeth could see Libby gazing at her anxiously. "Where did you put the resolutions?" she inquired in a concerned voice.

"They're safe here in my bag," Elizabeth said. "If only they help to convince the governor that he should give a pardon to Hester Vaughn!"

"Poor Hester!" Libby said sorrowfully.

"Poor Hester, indeed," Elizabeth echoed. "How many thousands of times has her tragic experience been repeated in the history of the world? How cruel and unjust that woman is invariably the one who must pay the dreadful penalty!"

When twenty years old, Hester Vaughn had come from England to Philadelphia with her husband, who soon deserted her. Finding work as a housemaid, she was seduced by her employer. When he discovered that she was pregnant, he discharged her. Alone and friendless, she gave birth in midwinter in an unheated attic room. For twenty-four hours she lay helpless and often unconscious, rousing at intervals to call for help. When discovered, she was in a dangerously weakened condition, and the infant was dead. Almost at once she was placed in prison, tried without proper defense, and sentenced to death for killing her newborn child, although there was no proof that she had done so.

Was not Hester Vaughn's seducer as guilty as Hester? Elizabeth asked in the columns of *The Revolution*. There should be equal moral standards for men and women.

Was it fair for a woman to be judged by an all-male jury? If there was so much stress laid on a trial by one's peers, should not women be judged by an all-female jury? Only women could understand the depths of Hester's difficulties. Only women, therefore, should make the laws that governed women, and they should continue to demand the ballot toward that end.

As for capital punishment—was it not barbarous and antiquated? Figures proved that it did not lessen crime. Surely there must be some humane method of helping criminals to turn from their wickedness and enter into lives of usefulness.

The Working Woman's Association, after listening to a dramatic recital of Hester Vaughn's story by the youthful orator, Anna Dickinson, sent two women, one of them a physician, to Philadelphia to investigate the case. They were convinced that Hester was innocent and worthy of help. At a large meeting in Cooper Union the Association passed a number of resolutions.

Now Elizabeth felt an almost sacred responsibility in carrying those resolutions to the governor of Pennsylvania. They demanded a new trial or unconditional pardon for Hester Vaughn. They went on to state that women should be tried by a jury of women, and that women should be able to take part in the making of laws. Finally they urged the abolishment of capital punishment.

The next day, during the interview at the governor's office, Elizabeth was not dismayed that he did not at once agree to grant a pardon to Hester Vaughn. A man in his position would want people to think that he and he alone had made the decision. He would need time to decide.

Later, when Elizabeth and her cousin visited the prison, they found Hester in a solitary cell with a narrow cot and one straight chair, gazing despondently at the unrelieved gray walls. Her soft brown hair was neat, her hands folded.

As the guard unlocked the door, she looked up, her eyes pools of anguish.

"We have come to help you," Elizabeth said, compassion flooding over her.

"That's good of you, ma'am," Hester said dully.

"We are trying to secure a pardon for you," Libby said.

"That's what those other ladies said," the young woman stated, "but I'm still here." She looked bleakly at the wall.

What could she say to bring this girl hope? Elizabeth wondered. She dared not promise her freedom. There was no guarantee that the governor would respond mercifully to the resolutions. If only she could penetrate Hester's deep despair.

"Would you like to tell us about yourself?" Elizabeth asked gently. "I understand that you are from England. Long ago I made a visit there. Perhaps I have been near your home."

Encouraged, Hester poured out her tale. Her family had been poor, and when a young man proposed marriage and emigration, she had gladly consented. In America everyone was rich, she had heard, and they would soon be so. But after landing her husband had left her without a penny, and she had nearly starved before finding work. Then her employer made improper advances.

"Why did you give in to him?" Elizabeth asked.

"I was afraid, ma'am. He said if I did as he wanted, I could keep on working. If not, he'd discharge me. And that's what he did anyway, as soon as he found out that I was in a family way." Hester burst into tears.

"But I didn't kill my baby, ma'am. I didn't. I was near dead myself by the time it was born, and too weak even to lift my head to look at the poor little thing."

Elizabeth patted her shoulder. "My dear, my dear, you must not despair. Somehow, someday, these guilty men will be brought to justice. Meanwhile you must be brave and courageous, and remember that there are thousands of women who know of your suffering and are determined to help you."

In her mind's eye she recalled the long succession of young girls whom she had befriended during past years. There had been numerous young servant girls, naïve and trusting. Might not any one of them have become involved in just such a situation as Hester Vaughn?

Elizabeth thought of the many friends of her daughters, even of Margaret and Harriot themselves. What if circumstances had placed them in a similar position? Her heart was wrung with pity for Hester and the thousands of other women who inhabited a world of double standards.

In cases of seduction, women, without exception, were branded as guilty, while the men got off scot-free. Changes must be made. Once the legal steps were taken, surely society's attitude would change, too.

But oh, how long it took to effect reforms! If only women had the vote. Surely they would ensure equal justice for all!

When the time for visiting Hester Vaughn had elapsed, Elizabeth and her cousin took leave of the pathetic young woman. The warden ceremoniously escorted them through the long corridors, and bowed low as they made their exit to the street and their waiting carriage.

As they rode through Philadelphia's busy streets, Elizabeth gave a long sigh. Libby threw her a questioning glance.

"I was just wishing that my old nurse could see us now," Elizabeth said. "Here we are, two snowy-haired matrons, the very picture of sober respectability. And yet we have been doing just what she punished me for when I was a child. She said then that it was highly improper for me to go to the jail and talk to the prisoners. I wonder what she would say if she were here today?"

"Probably that you hadn't changed very much," Libby said. Giving Elizabeth's hand a squeeze, she added, "Thank heaven you haven't!"

Back in New York, Elizabeth continued her plea for the pardon of Hester Vaughn, pointing out the need for equal justice for women, not only in the courts, but in society as well.

Some time later Hester Vaughn was pardoned, and allowed to return to England.

Elizabeth's relief was tinged by depression. She was thankful that Hester had been saved. But she grieved that the laws were unchanged. What of the countless women who were still under their power?

Determinedly she redoubled her efforts for woman suffrage. Only by the ballot could woman win her freedom.

19

ON THE PLATFORM

I'm sorry, ma'am, but the storm is so bad that all the trains are stalled. You cannot possibly get through to Maquoketa tonight."

From the lobby of the hotel in Lyons, Iowa, Elizabeth looked out at a snow-filled street. White drifts stretched from building to building, festooned the eaves, and covered the landscape as far as she could see. A strong wind blew frosty particles through the air.

"I am scheduled to speak there at eight o'clock this evening," she said. "Have you a sleigh, a pair of strong horses, and a reliable driver?"

"Oh, yes, ma'am," the hotel keeper said. "But a lady like you could not possibly stand a six-hour drive in this weather. You'd freeze to death."

A lady like me, indeed! Elizabeth thought. Did he think she was a fragile flower that must be kept in a hothouse? Or did he fear that her sixty-six years made her old and infirm? If this man had any idea of the rigors and dangers of a Lyceum lecture tour, he would change his tune in a hurry.

Pulling herself up to as much height as she could muster and putting on an imperious mien, she said, "Get the sleigh ready, if you please, and send a telegram to Maquoketa stating that I shall be there as arranged."

Then she went into the dining room and fortified herself with roast beef and apple pie. It might be her last meal, she thought grimly, if the man's prediction were true.

Half an hour later she climbed into the sleigh. It was difficult to move, swathed as she was in a flannel petticoat, woolen dress, jacket and coat, and, over all, her fur cloak and hood, with a heavy veil over her face to protect it from the wind. There was a heated oak plank for her feet, she noted thankfully.

As soon as she was seated, the hotel keeper threw a heavy double buffalo robe over her, enveloping her completely except for her head. He tied the two tails of the skins at the back of her neck. Ugh! What a rank odor! The next moment a blast of wind all but took her breath away. She'd be thankful for the buffalo robe, smell and all, she suspected, before the trip was over.

Three hours later Elizabeth began to wonder if she might not have made a mistake in judgment. Her body seemed to have lost all warmth. The oak plank was as frigid as her feet. The icy wind whipped her mercilessly. For miles she had seen nothing but an endless sea of snow.

Eight years ago, when she had decided to accept the Lyceum Lecture Bureau's invitation to become one of their featured speakers, she had realized that the assignment would not be easy. Her experience in Kansas had taught her that travel in the West was fraught with hardship.

The offer had come at a crucial time in the Stantons' family life. Elizabeth's work as editor of *The Revolution* had ended when Susan was forced to sell the newspaper in 1870 due to lack of funds. Henry's earnings as an attorney and editorial writer for the *New York Tribune* were adequate for the normal running expenses of their household, a considerable amount since the spacious home they had recently built in Tenafly, New Jersey, across the Hudson River from

New York City, was constantly filled with their own and their children's guests. The butcher's bill alone was a staggering sum.

The additional cost of college fees was more than they could afford. Yet both Elizabeth and Henry felt it important that their children have the opportunity of higher education. Just as they were wondering where the money was to come from, Elizabeth was asked to go on tour.

Since she would receive one hundred dollars or more each time she spoke, and the Bureau booked her appearances as closely together as possible, she should earn three to four thousand dollars for the eight months she would be on tour each year. As the most widely known woman speaker in the United States, she was expected to attract large audiences everywhere.

Henry and Elizabeth held long consultations. In the end they agreed that Elizabeth should accept. Her fees would pay for Theodore's education at Cornell, Margaret's at Vassar, and would ensure that Harriot and Robert might also enroll in college. During Elizabeth's absence, Amelia Willard would continue to run the household smoothly, as she had for many years.

"I only ask," Henry said, "that you take the same care for your health and safety that you would for any of us. God knows how deeply I'll miss you." He embraced her tenderly, adding, "I knew when we met that you were no ordinary woman!"

How thankful Elizabeth was to be able to offer her children the opportunity for college training that she herself had longed for so desperately and to give Henry some relief from his crushing financial load. Most of all she welcomed

the Lyceum tour as a means of spreading abroad the gospel
of women's freedom.

People paid a great deal more attention to a speaker on a
platform than they did to columns of print in a newspaper,
she had discovered. Many audiences came partly out of curi-
osity to see what kind of a woman Elizabeth Cady Stanton
was—and remained to become enthusiastic supporters of
women's rights.

Elizabeth stamped her feet up and down on the plank.
They felt like blocks of ice, devoid of feeling. Would she
and the driver never arrive at their destination? The hotel
manager had said the drive would take six hours. It seemed
more like an eternity at this moment.

Where was Susan now? Elizabeth wondered. Out in this
bitter weather, too? Susan had become a Lyceum lecturer,
also, and was off on her own whirl of engagements. It was
not easy, this circuit. Elizabeth often feared that Susan could
not endure the lack of sleep and regular meals, the frequent
delays and waits in drafty, dirty, railroad stations, the long
hours of standing on the lecture platform.

What a treat it was when their schedules coincided and
they had a few hours or a Sunday together. It was like a
feast, being able to talk over their disappointments and trials.
Best of all was the sharing of triumphs. How thrilled Susan
was when Elizabeth spoke in the Chicago Opera House, so
crowded that people sat in the aisles and on the stairs.

Often Susan and Elizabeth skipped briefly over their own
personal experiences to discuss the serious responsibilities
they shared.

In 1869 they had helped to form the National Woman
Suffrage Association with a group of women from nineteen

states who were delegates to the Equal Rights Association convention. They disagreed with its endorsement of the Fifteenth Amendment, which stated that the right to vote should not be denied on account of race, color, or previous condition of servitude. The word *sex* should rightfully have been included, they contended, and they formed a new organization to work primarily for a Sixteenth Amendment, enfranchising women. Elizabeth had been elected president by unanimous vote, and had been re-elected year after year. Susan was as firmly established, as a member of the executive committee. Letters flew back and forth between the two as they planned ways by which to secure the ballot for woman.

Although at first disturbed by the formation of a similar group called the American Woman Suffrage Association, fearing that it would weaken their own, they soon concluded that the second organization drew into membership many women of pronounced conservative views. Better that they make some effort for enfranchisement than none at all, Elizabeth thought.

Beneath the heavy buffalo skins, Elizabeth flexed her rigid fingers. She would like to put her hands up to her face to shield her stinging cheeks and nose, but she was imprisoned beneath the robe's heavy folds.

Twilight had fallen, and darkness was creeping over the land. How much farther had they to go? She shouted to the driver, but her words were torn away by the wind and failed to penetrate the shaggy fur cap pulled down over his ears.

Then, far off in the distance, Elizabeth saw a pinpoint of light. Relief flooded over her. To her annoyance a tear of thankfulness ran down her cheek—and instantly froze.

Half an hour later they entered the town to the joyful peal of church bells. Elizabeth was helped from the sleigh by an admiring group of citizens. For a few minutes she walked stiffly about, forcing her numb features into what she hoped was a smile, and replied to questions about her long, dangerous drive.

"I had agreed to speak here tonight, and so I shall," she said. "But why are the church bells ringing?"

"To let the people know that you had arrived safely," a man replied. "We were all very much concerned about you."

In spite of the severe weather, the auditorium was filled. Amazingly, Elizabeth had arrived just five minutes before the scheduled hour. Still in her many-layered traveling costume, except for her coat and cloak, and without an opportunity to eat a mouthful, she mounted the platform.

Tonight she would give her most popular lecture, "Our Girls." What a temptation to preface it with an account of the long, arduous ride across the prairie, and to point out that she was there on the platform only because from girlhood she had fought against the usual restrictions that weakened females, had engaged in regular exercise, healthful meals, a wholesome program of work and study, and had developed the strength as well as the courage to face situations that daunted many men.

If these people were as intelligent as she hoped, they would have the sense to know all that. Her very presence was proof of her stamina. And had she undergone any more than many of the women sitting here in the audience? Certainly some of them had suffered far worse dangers in their daily lives on the frontier.

"I wish," she began, "to pay tribute to the mothers who came here by long, tedious journeys, closely packed with restless children in emigrant wagons, cooking the meals by day and nursing the babies by night, while the men slept. Leaving comfortable homes in the East, they endured all the hardships of pioneer life, suffered with the men the attacks of Indians and the constant fear of savage raids, prairie fires, and devastating locusts. Man's trials, his fears, his losses, all fell on woman with double force, yet there is silence concerning the part woman performed in the frontier life of the early settlers."

Then she launched into her talk, telling how young girls start life with enthusiasm and eagerness to learn, often with wishes for a career, only to face repeated disappointments. She pleaded for a free and independent life for every girl, for clothing that would not hamper her movements, for education that would lead to her self-support, and for equal opportunity in business and the professions.

She made a plea for marriage as an equal partnership of spiritual and mental companionship. She announced her belief that the word *obey* should be deleted from the marriage ceremony.

And as always she reminded her listeners that woman's only sure way to equality and freedom was through enfranchisement.

"The world will talk to you of the duties of wives and mothers and housekeepers," she said, "but all these incidental relations should ever be subordinate to the greater fact of womanhood. You may never be wives, mothers, or housekeepers, but you will be *women*. Therefore labor for the grander and more universal fact of your existence."

Amid hearty applause Elizabeth concluded, uncomfortably conscious of the hall's high temperature and her many layers of clothing. Crowds of people pressed forward to shake her hand or to ask for her signature in their autograph books.

Here was a further opportunity to spread her beliefs. In one book she wrote: *Man and woman, a simultaneous creation*. And in another: *The masculine and feminine elements are equal in the Godhead*.

A young girl who smilingly presented a small album so strongly resembled Harriot that for a moment Elizabeth was swept by a wave of homesickness. What she would not give for a few hours with her own beloved family! Or to have Harriot accompanying her on this tour as she had on several occasions, trying out her budding oratorical skill. Hastily Elizabeth pushed the thought away. She must not indulge in selfish desires, but attend to the business at hand.

With her pen she inscribed in firm letters: *I am a citizen of the United States and demand the right to vote*. She returned the book to its wide-eyed owner, saying, "I hope that you will take this as your motto, my dear, and act upon it until we women achieve our goal."

When the crowd had dwindled, friendly citizens conducted her to a nearby house. In the guest chamber Elizabeth thankfully removed her flannel petticoat and fitted jacket. What a relief to shed some of her layers at least.

Downstairs she was reminded of her hunger by the sight of a table laden with delicacies. The weary little hostess, flushed from frequent trips between kitchen and dining room, was setting a crusty chicken pie on the table among an assortment of cakes and custards. She must have been cooking for days to prepare so much food, Elizabeth thought.

In a few minutes, when all were seated, the host turned to her and said, "Would you care to ask a blessing, Mrs. Stanton?"

Looking at the sober faces about her, many of them masculine, Elizabeth assented. She was sick and tired of watching pompous men spread out their hands over meals that hard-working women had prepared and listening to them giving thanks to the Lord as if every dish had come down from heaven piping hot and ready to eat.

In a clear, reverent tone, she said: "Heavenly Father and Mother, make us thankful for all the blessings of this life, and make us ever mindful of the patient hands that oft in weariness spread our tables and prepare our daily food. For humanity's sake, Amen."

Raising her eyes, Elizabeth noted the flurry of excitement about the table, and the beaming smile that lit her hostess's face. One of the joys of being invited to people's homes was watching a new pride and self-respect come into a woman's expression after the homage paid her in this blessing that Elizabeth had composed for just such occasions. That it lacked conformity with the usual petitions for grace bothered her not one whit. It was time that woman had some appreciation!

The following day, as was her custom, Elizabeth met with the women alone, and talked to them on "Marriage and Maternity."

"A true conjugal union," she said, "is the highest kind of human love—divine, creative in the realm of thought as well as in the material world. A man's love brings inspiration, completeness, and satisfaction into a woman's existence.

"It is not only wrong but harmful to accept the belief that sex is a crime, marriage a defilement, and maternity a bane. I have great faith in nature's promptings and the sincere love of men and women for each other.

"When I was young," she continued, "I knew no better than to have seven children in quick succession. When women have a voice in the laws, there will no longer be taboos attached to spreading information on how to avoid a too generous perpetuation of the race. What a blessing that will be to overburdened mothers."

She went on to warn that when marriage is not a true partnership based upon love and mutual consideration, the parties involved should have the option of dissolving their union without suffering the disgrace and ostracism attached to persons undergoing divorce.

As Elizabeth finished, a red-faced woman rose and cried, "You're a disgrace to talk about such subjects as the limiting of births and divorce. You deserve to be stoned out of town."

At her words such a clamor arose that Elizabeth was forced to hold up her hands for silence. In the quiet that followed a handsome, middle-aged matron stood. "It is high time that someone had the courage to discuss such vital matters. I believe we owe Mrs. Stanton our sincere thanks." There followed a burst of applause.

In the question period many women rose to ask for more information, and to relate cases of cruelty and sorrow. Elizabeth was struck anew by the powerless plight of her sex.

Then it was time for Elizabeth to bundle up and go off in

the sleigh for another long, bitterly cold drive to the next town where she was to give talks.

For three weeks she continued on, driving forty or fifty miles a day, and filling every engagement scheduled. On her return to Chicago she met in the lobby of her hotel two men who had been booked to precede her on the lecture tour.

"Where have you been?" they asked. "We have been waiting here for the railroads to resume service."

"I simply hired a sleigh and driver," Elizabeth said airily. "How could you strong men let a little thing like snow keep you from your objective?"

The men began to stammer excuses. Elizabeth smiled serenely. She knew exactly why the men had given up and she had persevered. They were lecturing solely for financial gain. She was impelled by a fierce and unremitting determination to elevate the status of woman.

That goal had given her strength and courage under every adverse condition. If only her struggle might result in victory!

20

EIGHTY YEARS AND MORE

On November 12, 1895, Elizabeth approached the breakfast table in her eight-room apartment on East Sixty-first Street in New York City. Although she had not slept as well as usual, she was completely dressed even so early in the day, with a fresh white lace collar on her black silk dress, and her snowy hair combed into a crown of curls high on her head.

Theodore came toward her, waving a newspaper. Two months ago he had arrived from France, where he had made his home for many years. What a help he had been in making arrangements for tonight's events.

Handing her the paper, he pulled out her chair, and said, "Just wait until you read *The Sun*!"

Across the table Margaret, who was now a widow and a student in a teachers course in physical training, smiled cheerily. "You're bringing glory to us all, Mother."

Robert, tall and portly, said, "For a woman you have done rather well, I must say!"

"Robert!" Elizabeth sputtered. "Must you tease me on my eightieth birthday?"

She was indeed all of eighty years old, and considered an old woman by most of the world. But inwardly she felt as excited and eager as when she was a girl. If only her body had retained the resiliency of her spirit!

Now, what was this article in *The Sun* that the children

were talking about? She picked up the journal and scanned the page. Instantly a line blazed out at her. *This is Stanton Day in New York.*

For a moment her hand trembled. She looked up at Theodore, leaning over her, and let her head rest for a moment on his arm.

"Oh, Ted," she burst out, "I have never felt so nervous in my life! Or so unfitted for the part I have to play!"

"Now, Mother," Theodore said in a comforting tone, "you've faced far more terrifying situations. You'll just have to go through this ordeal with your usual heroism." He patted her shoulder and sat down.

Slowly, for her eyesight was failing, Elizabeth took in the sense of the editorial. It was full of praise for her long career in elevating the status of women.

"Such praise is too much of a change for me," she said testily. "I've spent most of my life hurling thunderbolts at the established order for its subjugation of woman. How can you expect me to be calm and unruffled when I must change my role completely? I'm not accustomed to being patted on the head and told that I've done well."

Ever since Elizabeth had learned of the plans to celebrate her eightieth birthday with a grand affair in the New York Opera House, she had been nervous and apprehensive. The low, clear voice that she had used at countless gatherings had grown hoarse from overuse. Worn out, like its owner, she thought.

And recently she had had a fall from which she had not fully recovered. It hurt her pride to use a cane, especially in public. Why, oh, why had Susan evolved and engineered this plan for such an elaborate celebration?

If Elizabeth could have her way, she would rather spend the evening quietly at home with a group of old friends discussing significant events. She had half a mind to refuse to appear.

"But you must be there," Susan had stated with her usual firmness. "Don't you realize that all over the nation the supporters of woman suffrage will be gathering that same evening to celebrate your birthday with similar programs? Just listen to this invitation that has gone out to organizations from the National Council of Women!"

Proudly Susan read: "Believing that the progress made by women in the last half century may be promoted by a more general notice of their achievements, we propose to hold, in New York City, a convention for this purpose. As an appropriate time for such a celebration, the eightieth birthday of Elizabeth Cady Stanton has been chosen. Her half century of pioneer work for the rights of women makes her name an inspiration for such an occasion and her life a fitting object for the homage of all women."

Susan gave Elizabeth a stern look. "You wouldn't wish to mar such an event by your absence, would you?"

"You know that I would do anything in my power to help our cause," Elizabeth said. "Of course I shall be there."

But in the weeks preceding the event, Elizabeth had known many qualms. Suppose her voice should fail completely? Or that she should stumble and fall on her way to the podium? If only Henry were still living to stand by her, she might not feel so timorous. But Henry had died, as had her mother, her sister Tryphena, and many of her close friends. Susan, however, now a vigorous seventy-five, seemed as active and enthusiastic as ever.

Elizabeth's mind flew back to the years following the Lyceum Lectures. What a busy time she and Susan and Matilda Joslyn Gage had had in collaborating on *The History of Woman Suffrage*. The first volume had appeared in 1881, the second soon after, and the third in 1886. How they had ever managed to sort through the mass of material and present it in accurate, readable form, she would never know. Now Susan and Ida Husted Harper were working on Volume IV, occasionally asking Elizabeth for advice and information.

It was a satisfaction to know that the early struggles of women for their rights were now faithfully recorded by those who had been active in the movement. There were accounts of every meeting of the National Woman Suffrage Association, and of the American Woman Suffrage Association as well, thanks to Harriot, who had claimed that readers would think her mother and Susan were discriminating against the second organization if they omitted its history.

Elizabeth and Susan had been too weary to write another word. So Harriot had set to work diligently, giving in 106 pages a concise story of the establishment and progress of the American Woman Suffrage Association up to its merger with the National Association.

It had been a triumph for the cooperative nature of woman that in 1890 the two groups had united, forming the National American Woman Suffrage Association. For two years Elizabeth had served as president, then had resigned. It was time to let others have a turn at the responsibility and problems of leadership.

That Harriot would one day assume a position of leadership in the cause of woman suffrage, Elizabeth was certain.

She was helping to further the movement in England, and bringing up her daughter, Nora Blatch, now thirteen, in a regime unfettered by worn-out ideas of female propriety.

The maid placed a halved and segmented orange at Elizabeth's place. She picked up her spoon. What a treat to have fresh oranges for much of the year, thanks to efficient transportation. When she was a girl, an orange had been a luxury.

As always before an important speech, she had no appetite at all. It was important to keep up one's strength, though. She would eat her orange and some cereal, and then perhaps her stomach would calm a little.

Suddenly the door bell shrilled. The maid brought in a sheaf of telegrams. Theodore opened them and read them aloud. Congratulations on eighty years of significant accomplishment for woman's cause, they said. The wording was different, the messages the same.

All through the day people kept coming to the door. Some bore bouquets of flowers. Others brought baskets of fruits. A few left other gifts, such as autographed books. All the world, it seemed, knew that Elizabeth was eighty years old today, and wanted to wish her well.

Somehow she got through the morning and afternoon. Then it was time to dress in the new black satin evening gown made especially for the occasion, with its broad, elaborate collar of delicate, handmade lace, as snowy as her hair.

The drive through crowded avenues lighted by gas street lamps was nearly silent. Elizabeth was assailed by a terror such as she had never before known.

At last they reached the opera house, and entered through

a side entrance, going directly to a dressing room behind the stage. There was time enough only to pat her curls into place, and to fluff the lace at her throat. Then she was being helped onto the stage.

Elizabeth caught a glimpse of a background composed of thousands of white carnations. Set into it were red carnations spelling out the name Stanton. Ahead of her was a red plush chair festooned with red roses.

On one side stood dear Susan, a welcoming smile on her lined face. On the other was Mary Lower Dickinson, president of the National Council of Women, sponsors of the event. And all about were old friends and coworkers and members of her family.

This was not the fearsome ordeal Elizabeth had dreaded. This was a happy reunion with those she held most dear. Confidently she started forward, and from the crowded opera house came a roar of welcome. Amidst a tumult of applause, Elizabeth took her seat.

Incredulously she listened to the speakers' words of praise: "grateful recognition of the debt the present generation owes to the pioneers of the past . . ." "influence of Mrs. Stanton and Miss Anthony has permeated all departments of progress . . ." "to honor a noble woman . . ." "hearts brave enough to think, and tender enough to feel . . ." "half a century of struggle to lift humanity from bondage, and womanhood from shame . . ."

When it was time for Elizabeth to speak, she walked unsteadily to the podium. Suddenly a thunder of applause burst forth. The audience rose to its feet, cheering and clapping in a tumult of enthusiasm.

Trembling, Elizabeth looked out over the blurred faces. It was difficult to believe that this tremendous ovation was for her.

When the vast auditorium was quiet, she began, "I thank you all very much for the tributes of love, respect, and gratitude which have been sent to me in telegrams and letters and expressed in the presence of this great audience."

Now she must make very clear the fact that tonight's program would never be taking place except for the nobility of the cause that had been her life's work.

"I am well aware," she continued, "that all these public demonstrations are not so much tributes to me as an individual as to the great idea I represent—the enfranchisement of women."

The enfranchisement of women! How long before her dream should become a reality? she wondered. Every effort to amend the Constitution to give women their sacred right to the elective franchise had so far failed. In vain she and her faithful, dedicated coworkers had gathered signatures for endless petitions; in vain they had made countless speeches; in vain they had appeared before innumerable committees and legislative bodies.

Year after year their woman suffrage amendment had been introduced into Congress. Year after year the legislators in Washington had failed to pass the measure ensuring that "the right . . . to vote shall not be denied or abridged . . . on account of sex."

But had the work really been in vain? The right to vote for school committee members had been granted to women in half the states, in municipal elections in Kansas, and in all local and state elections in Wyoming, Utah, and Colorado.

Looking out at the thousands of people filling the opera house, Elizabeth knew with certainty that every ounce of effort had given some impetus to woman's liberation. Surely the complete equality of man and woman could not be far away. She and her friends in the movement had made a good beginning. The important thing was to persevere.

For seven years after her eightieth birthday celebration Elizabeth continued her efforts to improve the status of women. She kept on producing articles for newspapers and magazines. In 1895 and 1897 she published two volumes of the *Woman's Bible*, commentaries on the Scriptures intended to make readers question the theological doctrines derogatory to women. In 1898 she brought out her autobiography, *Eighty Years and More*, in the hope that her lifelong struggle for the rights of women might inspire others to work toward the same goal.

On October 25, 1902, only one day before her death, she composed an urgent plea to Theodore Roosevelt, President of the United States. In that last product of her pen Elizabeth Cady Stanton once again repeated the demand she had first made at Seneca Falls fifty-four years before, that the Constitution be amended to secure to the women of the United States their sacred right to the elective franchise.

AUTHOR'S NOTE

It is appropriate that this book about a pioneer advocate of the equality of men and women should have been completed a few days after March 22, 1972, when the Senate of the United States gave its approval to the Equal Rights Amendment. A backward look across more than a century reveals the long-existent need for such legal recognition and the debt owed by today's women to their great-grandmothers in the women's rights movement.

While attempting to reconstruct the highlights in Elizabeth Cady Stanton's career, I grew to admire wholeheartedly the courageous, dedicated, and witty woman whose thinking was far in advance of her time. What a privilege it must have been to know her! And how I would like to share with readers every facet of her vibrant personality that came to light in my research.

From Mrs. Stanton's own pen have come most of the facts that form the framework of this book. The volume of her written work is evidence of the discipline and dedication that impelled her to strive unremittingly for the cause of women's liberation despite the rigorous demands of home and family.

The public life of Elizabeth Cady Stanton is recorded in the first three volumes of *The History of Woman Suffrage* (1881–1922, 6 vols.), congressional and state legislative documents, official woman suffrage statements and appeals—all of which were chiefly of her composition—and the lectures, pamphlets, and numerous articles—

which were entirely of her authorship—in a wide variety of newspapers and magazines.

Mrs. Stanton's private life is presented in her autobiography, *Eighty Years and More* (1898), which was revised and edited by Theodore Stanton and Harriot Stanton Blatch and republished in two volumes under the title *Elizabeth Cady Stanton As Revealed in Her Letters, Diary, and Reminiscences* (1922).

Further information about Mrs. Stanton and her family is given in *Challenging Years* by Harriot Stanton Blatch and Alma Lutz (1940).

"One of the most prolific, meticulous, and articulate chroniclers of American feminism," Alma Lutz has written a sympathetic and detailed work entitled *Created Equal: A Biography of Elizabeth Cady Stanton 1815–1902* (1940). Mrs. Stanton also figures in other books by Alma Lutz: *Susan B. Anthony: Rebel, Crusader, Humanitarian* (1959); *Emma Willard; Pioneer Educator of American Women* (1964); and *Crusade for Freedom: Women in the Antislavery Movement* (1968).

Letters in Mrs. Stanton's handwriting give proof of her generous nature as well as of her daring spirit and lively wit. Long treasured by the recipients, many of these messages are now housed in special collections, two of which I used extensively—the Arthur and Elizabeth Schlesinger Library at Radcliffe College and the Sophia Smith Collection at Smith College. I am grateful for having had access to those collections.

To Helen and Arnold Barben and Shirley Patterson of the Seneca Falls Historical Society I owe a special debt for permission to go through the society's file of Stanton papers and to view Mrs. Stanton's desk and piano among other memorabilia in the Historical Museum. Above all I appreciate Mr. and Mrs. Barben's kindness in conducting me to such key points as the Stanton house, the Hunt mansion in nearby Waterloo, and the Methodist Chapel where Elizabeth Cady Stanton made the historic first demand for the enfranchisement of women.

For historical data on the Cady family and places significant in Mrs. Stanton's girlhood, such as the Johnstown Academy, the Courthouse, and the former Cady home, I wish to thank Nina Sloan Bovee of the Johnstown Public Library. In its collection are copies of *The History of Woman Suffrage*, one of which bears on the flyleaf the following inscription:

> These three volumes are largely the work of dear Mrs. Stanton—and I place them in the Johnstown Free Library in memory of the ten years that we spent compiling them—this vol. III was compiled at Johnstown—she living with Mrs. Eaton and Mrs. Bayard in the old home—and I boarding with Mrs. Henry a block away.
>
> SUSAN B. ANTHONY
> Rochester, N.Y.

Nov. 8, 1905

Among the many libraries whose collections I consulted, I am grateful to the Boston Public Library for the extended use of out-of-print publications necessary to this work.

And for their day-to-day support, encouragement, and cheerful furnishing of information, I wish to offer sincere thanks to my loyal friends of the Melrose Public Library.

M. S. C.

Melrose, Massachusetts
March 1972

INDEX

About the Author

MARY STETSON CLARKE was born and brought up in Melrose, Massachusetts, and after graduating from Boston University, worked on a Boston newspaper until her marriage to Edwin L. Clarke, an electrical engineer. She and her husband then lived near New York City, where she attended Columbia University and wrote feature articles for various publications.

After the Clarkes returned to Melrose, and while their son and two daughters were in their teens, Mrs. Clarke began writing historical novels for young people, based on intensive research. Her books include *The Limmer's Daughter*, *The Glass Phoenix*, and *Piper to the Clan*.

Bloomers and Ballots grew out of Mrs. Clarke's study of the early days of the women's rights movement. Indignant at the injustices suffered by women, she decided to chronicle the story of Elizabeth Cady Stanton, the dauntless crusader whose demand for women's right to vote was the beginning of today's liberation movement.